Sharing the Gospel
So People Will
Listen ... and
Respond!

"Vince is a master in communicating the good news of Jesus. Along with *Miracle Conversions* and *Stories from the Street*, this book completes an important trilogy on evangelism. Written in everyday language with gripping stories and sprinkled with humor, *you* will be inspired to share the Gospel so people will listen and respond!"
**Graham Powell** – Center Mountain Ministries, Canada

"Vince Esterman has earned the right to publish a book on this subject. His passion for soul winning has increased, not diminished with the passing years. I have watched him in action on the streets of Paris. I have seen the way that indifferent, sceptical university students have been captivated by his presentations. Vince's writing style is enthralling, the material is practical and the principles are easy to grasp. The short topical sections make for easy reading and allow for stop/start digesting. The illustrations are apt and gripping. Vince is a great storyteller, but all his stories pack a punch. This book has a powerful, liberating and practical message for individual Christians, for pastors and for the whole Church body."
**Rev Trevor Chandler** – *Founder/Chairman*
Christian Life Churches International, Australia

"Vincent Esterman is a man on a mission! He combines Australian inventiveness with French passion and it is a potent combination. He and his wife Denise have been consistent, faithful leaders in France for a generation. What I respect most about him is that he never flags in his zeal to love and win people who don't know Christ. As such, he is one of the great encouragers of the body of Christ today. I strongly recommend this book."
**Charlie Cleverly** – *Rector*, St. Aldate's, Oxford

"I believe we need to carry the contagious virus of the good news, but our message *must* be simple, obtainable and relevant. In this book Vince Esterman is able to combine passion with practical application to convince you that you can communicate this message. It is time for ordinary people to carry this extraordinary message of Jesus and have a confidence it will work. This book will equip you to do it."
**Rachel Hickson** – *Director*, Heartcry Ministries

# Sharing the Gospel So People Will Listen ... and Respond!

Vince Esterman

New Wine Press

New Wine Ministries
PO Box 17
Chichester
West Sussex
United Kingdom
PO20 6YB

Copyright © 2005 Vince Esterman

All rights reserved. No part of this publication may be reproduced, stored in a retrieval system, or transmitted in any form or by any means, electronic, mechanical, photocopying or otherwise, without the prior written consent of the publisher. Short extracts may be used for review purposes.

Scripture quotations are taken from the following versions of the Bible:

NASB – New American Standard Bible. Copyright © 1960, 1962, 1963, 1968, 1971, 1972, 1973, 1975, 1977, 1995 by The Lockman Foundation.

NKJV – The Holy Bible, New King James Version. Copyright © 1982 by Thomas Nelson Inc.

ISBN 1-903725-55-0

Typeset by CRB Associates, Reepham, Norfolk
Cover design by CCD, www.ccdgroup.co.uk
Printed in Malta

# Contents

| Chapter 1 | Oh, What a Message! | 7 |

## PART 1:
## Key Issues

| Chapter 2 | The Gospel – Is it Good News, Really? | 21 |
| Chapter 3 | The Secret of Success | 33 |
| Chapter 4 | Getting People to Listen . . . and to Respond | 45 |
| Chapter 5 | Being Well Received | 61 |

## PART 2:
## The Good Samaritan

| Chapter 6 | Why Did Jesus Choose a Samaritan as the Hero of His Story? | 75 |
| Chapter 7 | Feeling for People | 83 |
| Chapter 8 | Oil, Wine and Donkeys | 93 |
| Chapter 9 | The Inn for Injured Travellers | 103 |
| Chapter 10 | Evangelists and Pastors Getting on | 115 |
| Chapter 11 | Who Pays? | 125 |

## PART 3:
### *Your Church Could Become a Soul-Winning Church*

*Chapter 12*    Your Church Could Become a Soul-Winning Church    135

*Chapter 13*    Honouring Evangelists    147

                About the Author    157

# Oh, What a Message!

"Don't do too many bad things and go to church." That was my weak response to someone who asked me what you had to do to become a Christian. Despite having been raised in a traditional church and having had a life-changing experience of Jesus at age fifteen, I did not understand the Gospel and deep down I knew it. Having the symbol of the cross is one thing. Being able to preach its message is quite another.

The Gospel is simply God's declaration of His love for people and the cross of Calvary is like an arrow fired from heaven to which this declaration is attached. There has never been anything like it in all of human history. Literary greats have not been able to match its beauty and no politician has ever equalled its all-embracing promises. It is a message of love and forgiveness, of fellowship and friendship with God, of never-ending life, of transcendent power and partaking in heaven's glory. It is a message that reaches deep into the human heart and lifts man to unimaginable heights. Where there is no hope, the Gospel gives a future. Where there is no meaning, the Gospel brings a purpose. It stirs the spirit in a man and shows him clearly that he is not a highly-evolved animal, but a divinely-fashioned creation.

The God of heaven had something to do on the earth and something to say to man. The Good News of Jesus Christ is that message. All religions have sacred books and holy men to explain them, but the Gospel brings with it the power to save – and for a drowning man, nothing else matters. Because it is preached, proud men become humble, bad men become good and broken lives are healed. It sorts people out! Who knows who will be the next person to receive grace to respond to it? Like satellite beams showing little respect for national boundaries, heaven's message cuts across all social barriers. The rich stand next to the poor singing, "Amazing grace, how sweet the sound, that saved a wretch like me".

Every emotion known to man has been awakened through its preaching: regret for past sins, indignation for lost years, passion for what is right and of course, joy – *"joy inexpressible and full of glory"* as Peter put it (1 Peter 1:8 NASB). Those who are bored to tears with life, on receiving it are moved to tears. This heavenly message takes men out of valleys and places them on hilltops and looking up, they go higher still till they live among the stars.

Each star is like a promise made by God, a nightly reminder that there is another life and another way to live your life.

Some preach the benefits of Amway or plastic Tupperware. If eternity were to be spent in the kitchen then no doubt their message would be mine. Others preach the virtues of wrinkle-reducing facial creams or hair restorers preventing baldness. If I were condemned to endless living with an ageing body then I would also preach these messages. But my message speaks of ageless bodies before a throne of glory and preach it I will, while I have breath.

The Gospel is a beautiful story that begins with a baby in a stable. God becomes a child and lives and grows amongst us. He will eat our food, play our games, walk our roads and feel our tiredness. He teaches like no man has ever taught and when sick people touch Him, they are healed. It sounds too good to be true, yet true it is.

When they nail Him to a cross it all seems to go horribly wrong and confused disciples flee. But things are still on track. The message is taking shape, the story is being written. In the invisible world, doors open and curtains of separation are torn down as, single-handedly, Jesus of Nazareth, the one they call the Christ, takes on and defeats hordes of dark angels. Three days and no more. Death, for Him, is so brief, so temporary. He rises from the grave, the marks of the nails still in His hands, but He has now changed. To see Him, your eyes have to be opened and when they are, light rushes in and every shadow is dispelled. It is all that Isaiah prophesied when he wrote, *"The people who walk in darkness will see a great light"* (Isaiah 9:2 NASB).

"Love is all you need" the song goes. Yes, but we all know

that love often disappoints. Not so the love preached through the Gospel. This is the capital "L" kind of love, not the kind you see on the big screens that lasts for an hour and a half. God's love for me! I could shout it from the rooftops, "There is a God and He loves me!" But the Gospel message is not so much that He loves *me* but that He loves *you* and wants you with Him for ever.

Life is full of events that help me understand what Jesus has done for me. Once I was waiting at Cardiff International Airport to catch a flight back to Paris. My Frequent Flyer card doesn't normally allow me to get into the airport executive lounges, but there have been odd times when it's worked. So I went up to the welcome desk of the lounge and asked if I could get in with my card. Beyond the young woman at reception I could see all the "privileged" travellers enjoying the comfort of the lounge and all the good free food and I wanted to join them. The woman checked my card and said, "I'm terribly sorry, sir, but you can't get in with that card." Excluded yet again and powerless to do anything about it, condemned to the departure lounge where all the food had to be paid for! As I was glumly putting my card back into my wallet, the man next to me said to the lady, "I have the right card and I am entitled to bring in a guest." The woman replied," Yes, sir, that's right." Smiling to me he said, "Then this man is my guest" and in I went! Thank God for Jesus, otherwise I would be condemned to standing outside the gates of heaven with the wrong card.

Our Gospel message is that Jesus has the right card and we're going in as His guest. And dear friends, in heaven all the food will be free!

## Bible images of an evangelist

The title of this book is *Sharing the Gospel So People Will Listen . . . and Respond!* We are ultimately talking about successful evangelism and becoming effective evangelists, but do we really understand the ministry of the Evangelist? Reading through the New Testament there are many "allusions" to other professions whenever an evangelist is mentioned. I like to think of the evangelist as:

▶ *A journalist*: He is a news presenter.

> "And how shall they preach unless they are sent? As it is written,
> 'How beautiful are the feet of those who preach the gospel
> of peace,
> Who bring glad tidings of good things.'"
> (Romans 10:15 NKJV)

▶ *A postman*: He delivers God's invitation to heaven's feast.

> "Again he sent out other slaves saying, 'Tell those who have been invited, "Behold, I have prepared my dinner."'"
> (Matthew 22:4 NASB)

▶ *An ambassador*: He is the official representative of a king in a foreign land.

> "Therefore, we are ambassadors for Christ, as though God were making an appeal through us; we beg you on behalf of Christ, be reconciled to God."
> (2 Corinthians 5:20 NASB)

▶ *A farmer*: He works a field, sows it and brings in a harvest.

*"And He was saying to them, 'The harvest is plentiful but the laborers are few; therefore beseech the Lord of the harvest to send out laborers into His harvest.'"*

(Luke 10:2 NASB)

▶ *A fisherman*: Unsaved people are like fish and evangelists are sent to catch them.

*"And He said to them, 'Follow me, and I will make you fishers of men.'"*

(Matthew 4:19 NASB)

▶ *A plumber*: Salvation is seeing living water flow into the hearts of people.

*"But whoever drinks of the water that I shall give him will never thirst. But the water that I shall give him will become in him a fountain of water springing up into everlasting life."*

(John 4:14 NKJV)

▶ *An electrician*: The evangelist channels power to produce light.

*"For God, who said, 'Light shall shine out of darkness,' is the One who has shone in our hearts to give the Light of the knowledge of the glory of God in the face of Christ."*

(2 Corinthians 4:6 NASB)

- *A rescuer*: Coastal and mountain regions have professional rescue services for those who get lost or who are caught up in difficulty.

  *"For the Son of Man has come to seek and to save that which was lost."*

  (Luke 19:10 NASB)

- *A taxi driver*: The evangelist picks people up and brings them to God's house and to the feast He has prepared.

  *"And the master said to the slave 'Go out into the highways and along the hedges, and compel them to come in, that my house may be filled.' "*

  (Luke 14:23 NASB)

- *A diplomat*: He associates with many different kinds of people, knows how to relate to them and win them over.

  *"To the weak I became weak, that I might win the weak; I have become all things to all men, so that I may by all means save some."*

  (1 Corinthians 9:22 NASB)

- *A midwife*: The evangelist is not necessarily the father of the child in the womb of a pregnant woman, but will, however, be the one who assists with new birth.

  *"Jesus answered and said to him, 'Truly, truly, I say to you, unless one is born again he cannot see the kingdom of God.' "*

  (John 3:3 NASB)

▶ *A guide*: Strangers to a city or a region appreciate a guide who knows the way and who can take them where they want to go.

*"And he said, 'How can I, unless someone guides me?' And he asked Philip to come up and sit with him."*

(Acts 8:31 NKJV)

▶ *A boiler room operator*: Evangelists light fires in hearts and make them burn with desire for God.

*"They said to one another, 'Were not our hearts burning within us while He was speaking to us on the road, while He was explaining the Scriptures to us?'"*

(Luke 24:32 NASB)

▶ *A father*: This, of course, is not a profession but it is, nonetheless, the role of an evangelist. He not only delivers the babies of others but fathers his own.

*"For if you were to have countless tutors in Christ, yet you would not have many fathers, for in Christ Jesus I became your father through the gospel."*

(1 Corinthians 4:15 NASB)

▶ *A guest*: This also is not a profession but a role. The evangelist will need to respond to the openhearted welcome of hosts.

*"Whatever house you enter, first say, 'Peace be to this house' ... Stay in that house, eating and drinking what they give you ..."*

(Luke 10:5, 7 NASB)

Yes, the evangelist is one of God's specialists, yet his field of work is multifaceted. His training will come through his own reading of the Bible and clearly, the teaching and example of experienced evangelists, men of God who have proven ministries and whose fruit speaks for itself. Yet, the ministry of the evangelist is learnt "as you go", the Holy Spirit shaping and fashioning a life, placing in the person the heart of God for the lost and the understanding of the way that leads to the human soul. He not only grasps biblical truth, but knows how to apply it very personally to the one who is searching for God.

It is a fascinating life; one that allows us to be on the front row watching God's stage as He confirms the message we bear. If you want to see God at work this is the place to be!

## Passionate about *The Passion*

It was the start of the Easter holiday weekend and I knew that many students would be away on holidays. Paris is well known for its April showers and that day was no exception. Rain threatened and temperatures were down. But what was really weighing on my decision to take my sketchboard out on the streets in front of the university was that it also happened to be my fiftieth birthday and I was very much looking forward to the "surprise" dinner my wife was organising that evening. Everything in me and around me cried out for cancellation of my weekly evangelism. However, because it is often the case that my best days are those when I feel the least inclined, I went out anyway.

I was right about the students: there were few around and I knew that gathering a crowd would be difficult. It was also at this time that the controversy over Mel Gibson's film, *The Passion of the Christ* was raging in France and I was trying to make the most of it.

At the end of one of my stories a young man remained behind. This one wanted to talk. "What's your name?" I asked. "Eddy" came back the reply. "Say, Eddy, have you seen *The Passion of the Christ?*" I asked. I could hardly believe what came next. This first-year university student, majoring in modern literature, had been a self-confessed atheist. His only contact with religion was Islam through his non-practising Tunisian father. At twenty years of age he had rejected any possibility of God. Incredibly, his first assignment at the beginning of the year had been to study the Gospel of Matthew as a literary work. This, in itself, is hard to believe for a French radical university. Eddy had never read the Bible but was immediately impacted by what he read. So when Mel Gibson's film was finally released in France after much opposition he went straight to the cinema. The first time he saw it was with a friend of his, a Satanist, who laughed his way through every terrible scene. But Eddy was not laughing. His soul had been deeply stirred by the suffering and death of Jesus. Who could he turn to for help? Who could he speak with? Then he remembered having seen a pastor with a sketchboard on a Friday afternoon in front of the university entrance. The day I nearly didn't go out was the day Eddy came looking for me.

We talked about the film and about Jesus. That Sunday, Easter Sunday, Eddy was in church and when I made the altar call for salvation, he was the first one out, saying later that he felt

God place His hand on his life. The following week he was back on the streets where we had met, but this time to witness to other students. And witness he did, powerfully sharing what Jesus had done for him. In the days that followed, he received a Pentecost-like experience of the baptism with the Holy Spirit and the day we baptised him in water the glory of God was literally over this young man. Before they stopped showing *The Passion*, Eddy and I, just the two of us, went to see it, this the third time for me and the fourth for him. We were ready for the end and as people stayed stunned in their seats, we slipped out onto the streets to be in position to hand them all an invitation to the special Sunday visitor's morning on the theme of "The Passion of the Christ ... WHY?"

Eddy has a brilliant mind and a love for the Word of God. Recently we were having lunch together at McDonald's and he said to me, "I'd like to become a doctor (the French word for teacher) of the Word." He thought for a moment then added, "What's a doctor of the Word?" I just smiled and inwardly thanked God for it all.

# PART ONE

## Key Issues

# The Gospel – Is it Good News, Really?

If only more had been written on the ministry of the evangelist in the New Testament! Apostles, prophets, teachers and pastors (shepherds) are often referred to in the Gospels and epistles alike, though perhaps each would wish that even further light had been shed on his particular ministry. Only one evangelist is named as such and while apostles do evangelise significant geographical areas, the planting of churches and the subsequent need to structure and care for them, distinguish this ministry from that of the evangelist.

It is true that we have a perfect example of the ministry of the evangelist in the person and work of Jesus Himself. He preached everywhere the good news of the Kingdom of God and on many occasions won individuals and sometimes even whole towns to His powerful life-changing message. Yet, Jesus is Jesus. It would no doubt be easier for a would-be evangelist to identify with ministries less perfect. And in any case, Jesus was never just an evangelist, being as well a brilliant teacher, a tender-hearted shepherd, a sharp prophet and having promised to build His Church, merited the title the author of Hebrews gives Him as Apostle (Hebrews 3:1). You become a difficult ministry model for others when you are all five rolled into one!

Keeping these limitations in mind, let's see what we can glean from the information we do have. Literally, from the Greek word translated "evangelist" we have a simple definition: "one who announces good news". Two immediate issues come to mind. Is the Gospel really good news for people and how should it be announced?

## Good news for whom?

Everyone loves getting good news when it's really good news. But there is good news and news that is good. If someone were to say to a European, "The drought in California has finally been broken" is that good news? Of course it is! I've lived through genuine drought conditions in Australia where crops are ruined, animals are left to die for lack of fodder and water, huge expanses of bush land and forests are devastated by bushfires and rivers become dust bowls. Droughts are terrible things, so when someone says to me that the drought in California is broken, I am very pleased for everyone involved.

However, if I were to say to that same European, "You have

just inherited one million Euros (approximately $1,200,000)" what impact would this news have on him? Let's be quite honest now. Which do you think he would prefer to hear? Which news would create the greater response in him? Obviously, the one million Euros! Now for him, that *is* good news! For this European, the drought broken in California is just news that is "good" ... for someone else.

This is the heart of the problem with how we present the Gospel. When I say to an unsaved person, "I have good news to share with you: Jesus died for the forgiveness of your sins," generally speaking, what kind of impact will this have on him? The "California drought" type impact or the "one million Euros" type impact? To the Western mind it will often be the former.

The same problem arises with our testimony. If I share with an unsaved person, "Jesus saved me and freed me from my past," he may listen with respect, but he is likely to have the same attitude towards me as if I had said, "I've just received a pay rise." It's good news for me, but not for him. However, I would get a totally different response if I said to him, "Listen, I've just been speaking with your boss and he told me that he will be giving *you* a huge pay rise." Now I would have his interest! This is not news that is good. It's good news!

So, for our news to be good news for the person we are speaking to, our message must begin with him or her.

## Starting with the other person's needs

In Acts 8 we find a hot evangelist at work. It's Philip and we know that he, at least, is a real evangelist, as he is the only one identified as such in the New Testament. He has just come out of the Samarian revival and has the challenge of leading an African Jew to respond to the Gospel message. His goal is to preach Jesus to this high-ranking Ethiopian so he chooses the best possible passage from the Old Testament scriptures to do so. It's Isaiah 53 and he's immediately into it, explaining how,

> "He was wounded for our transgressions,
> He was bruised for our iniquities;
> The chastisement for our peace was upon Him,
> And by His stripes we are healed."
>
> (Isaiah 53:5 NKJV)

Brilliant, straight to the heart of our message! Yet Philip did not start here because it raised the question of the cross of Jesus, nor because it was the best passage of Scripture a New Testament evangelist had at his disposal at that time. The reason for Isaiah 53 is obvious. This is where the Ethiopian was and it was concerning this passage that he wanted answers:

> "Please tell me, of whom does the prophet say this? Of himself or someone else?"
>
> (Acts 8:34 NASB)

The answer that Philip gives to this question is very good news to the man who asked it.

Sometime later, Paul is in Athens surrounded by philosophers. This is the same Paul who had written to the nearby Corinthians that he knew nothing but the cross of Christ. Yet, confronted by these hard-nosed Western thinkers, Paul does not start with Isaiah 53. It doesn't get a mention. He begins with them:

> "Men of Athens, I observe that you are very religious in all respects. For while I was passing through and examining the objects of your worship, I also found an altar with this inscription, 'TO AN UNKNOWN GOD.' Therefore what you worship in ignorance, this I proclaim to you."
>
> (Acts 17:22–23 NASB)

Paul had their full attention. "We're going to learn something with this guy! This should be good," they think. And they are right, it sure is good. Good news, that is.

Let me give you an example of how I talk to people about God. On a weekly basis I find myself surrounded by French thinkers, students and professors of the Jussieu and Sorbonne universities in Paris. I've never tried my hand with Greeks, but I'm confident that the French philosophers would be at least on par with them. After all, to complete their high school education, the very first test that they will have to sit for to pass their Baccalaureat is a two-hour exam on philosophy. So this is what I might say to them: "You probably have trouble believing in God. That's perfectly understandable given the kind of education you've had. And if you've had trouble believing in God, then you've probably had trouble believing that God could love you sufficiently to want to make a difference in your life. So here's what I'll do. I know that God loves you, so I'm going to ask Him to do something special for you in the next three days to start to get you thinking." I'm amazed at the looks on the students faces when I say this. I've started with them and I'm telling them to expect God to also start with them. You can be absolutely sure that if anything happens to them over the ensuing three days, they will not be able to shrug it off easily. It could only be good news for them one way or the other.

## Come to the feast

If you ask a person who has the ministry gift of teaching what he understands to be the Gospel, he will no doubt give you quite a detailed explanation beginning with Adam's sin in the Garden of Eden, moving on to Abraham's promise of blessing, Moses delivering Israel from Egypt and receiving the law, Israel's wanderings in the wilderness, the promised land, David and the kings, the prophets rebuking the people for their rebellion, John the Baptist, the birth of Jesus, the Cross, the Resurrection and Ascension followed by Pentecost. To round it off, they might add a little early Church history and the return of Jesus to usher in the end of the age. If you ask an evangelist what he understands to be the Gospel, he might reply with just one word, "Come!" This is why teachers and evangelists don't always understand each other. For the teacher, grasping God's plan of redemption is vital before anyone can legitimately be saved. For the evangelist, coming to Jesus will need to be followed by teaching about what He has accomplished for man. Teachers teach while evangelists call.

Getting this straight is vital if evangelists are to accomplish the ministry to which they have been called. God's plan of redemption and the Gospel are related but distinct messages. Redemption is God's plan for man to be reconciled to Himself. The Gospel is the invitation to personally receive God's grace and be reconciled. Explaining redemption gives understanding but sharing the Gospel seeks a response.

## Preaching bad news

Much evangelism in the past has tended to be "negative", at least in its initial approach to man. Because sin is real and ever present, some evangelists feel that it is their responsibility to expose and denounce evil in the lives of people and in society generally. Perhaps this negativity has been inspired by Peter's exhortation to the assembled crowd on the day of Pentecost to flee from this perverse generation. In any case, their message is far from good news for the hearers. If you listen to them, you might think that everyone is an adulterer, consumed with his or her own ego and interested in only one thing, money. I admit that many people today *are* like this. But what is the message communicating? Bad news. It is so very different when your approach is one of inviting people to a feast.

## Festive parables

Two of Jesus' parables, similar in content, deal with an invitation to a feast. They are found in Matthew 22 and Luke 14. God throws a party and His servants go out with the invitation to ensure that the festive dinner is a success. Perhaps we don't know everything about what we will do in heaven when we finally get there, but one thing is certain, we will be eating at a wedding feast (Revelation 19:9). This is the Kingdom of God. The success of the dinners in both parables was directly due to the work of the servants of the king and master: "Come, for everything is ready now," they said to the guests.

How often the invitation to come to God, and more specifically to Jesus in the New Testament, brought radical change to those who responded:

- To the rich young ruler the Saviour said, *"Sell what you have ... come, follow Me"* (Matthew 19:21 NKJV).
- To the disciples He said, *"Let the little children come to Me"* (Mark 10:14 NKJV).
- To the two disciples of John, Jesus said, *"Come and see"* (John 1:39 NKJV).
- To the Samaritan woman Jesus invited, *"Call your husband, and come here"* (John 4:16 NKJV).
- To the crowd gathered for the last day of the feast, Jesus cried out with a Gospel invitation, *"If anyone is thirsty, let him come to Me and drink"* (John 7:37 NASB).
- To the hesitant disciple Jesus said, *"Follow me, and allow the dead to bury their own dead"* (Matthew 8:22 NASB).
- And who can forget that beautiful invitation from Jesus, *"Come to Me, all who are weary and heavy-laden ..."* (Matthew 11:28 NASB).

The "Come and follow" invitation portrays God's real desire to bring outsiders of all categories into the household of faith. For any outsider who realises that he or she is one, this news is truly good news.

## God sees an individual

A major life insurance company in the USA brought in all its agents for a motivational convention in its New York headquarters. Hundreds from across the country gathered to hear bright, witty speakers stir them to see big and to climb to greater heights. They would take America and after that, the whole world! There was a buzz in the air between sessions and conversations during the coffee breaks were animated. While the delegates strategised, one young agent from California was at work in the building. During the three days, he managed to sell insurance policies to the lift operator, the hairdresser on the ground floor and a waiter in the company restaurant. While everyone was thinking big, one agent was thinking right. Succeeding in the insurance business is being able to sell one more policy to one more person.

That's the problem with too much hype about taking cities for God, reaching nations, seeing revival in Europe etc. It's big thinking and very visionary but, before God sees nations, He sees individuals.

> "For what profit is it to a man if he gains the whole world, and loses his own soul?"
>
> (Matthew 16:26 NKJV)

The Gospel is not an invitation to a nation but to an individual. Nations are not invited to the heavenly banquet, individuals are, and those who respond become God's holy nation.

I was in the street one day with my sketchboard doing my "How much does it cost?" message. I get the public involved by asking them to tell me the cost of different items or activities I put forward. "A young man wants to take out his girlfriend to the cinema," I began. "How much does it cost? Don't forget coffee and ice cream." Someone called out, "25 Euros." I went on, "The young man wants to declare his love for his girl, so he brings her flowers. How much does a bouquet cost?" Girls seem to know more than boys about the cost of flowers. One called out, "10 Euros."

"The girlfriend is very touched by the young man's declaration of love. She loves him too, so they begin to talk about marriage. How much does a beautiful wedding cost?" As I was telling the story, the crowd had gradually built up but no one seemed able to answer me. "Professionals estimate that you need around 8,000 Euros for all the expenses," I explained. Onlookers wondered where all this was leading to. "To pay for your wedding you can use your credit card, but not for a happy marriage," I argued. "Now a happy marriage, how much does that cost?" The tone of the message changed and the crowd again had no answer. "That's the whole problem," I added. "We all need happiness, but no shop sells a kilo of happiness. You can't buy it anywhere." I had everyone's attention. I could read their thoughts, "This man talks sense."

In the crowd in front of me was a group of teenage girls who initially had joked around, but who now were listening intently. I pressed home the advantage. "A seat in a cinema costs 8 Euros, but how much is a place in heaven?" Surprised and thoughtful looks came back at me. "Well, a place in heaven can't be bought. You can only go if you have a personal invitation. God has made out an invitation with your name on it and sent it to you. Have you received it?" I asked my street congregation. The first girl said indignantly, "No, I haven't!" The next one said, "I haven't either", but the third one was the surprise packet for me. She said, "Yes, I have received it." I immediately thought that she must have been from a Christian family. "When did you receive God's invitation to you?" I asked. "Just now," she replied, "while listening to you." Her answer brought a tear to the eye of this seasoned street evangelist. My punch-line seemed superfluous now, "Well, you received it because when God sends you your personal invitation to come to heaven, He doesn't fax it, mail it, or e-mail it. He just sends it heart-to-heart."

The Gospel was really good news for this young lady. As yet, of course, she didn't understand redemption, but she was responding to God's loving invitation to her.

# 3

# The Secret of Success

Hair is an amazing feature. You can curl it, dye it, gel it, shape it, plait it and, if you don't like it, you can shave it all off and let it grow back naturally. For most of us, our hair will not have an ultimate bearing on the outcome of our lives – unless, perhaps, you have such a stunning head of hair that people want to photograph you. For Samson however, it was different. Long hair was the reason for his strength and he was the only one to understand the secret of his success – until he told it to Delilah with tragic consequences.

Successful people have secrets and fundamental reasons why they have succeeded. The apostle Paul was one such person. Like Samson he had remarkable strength. Perhaps not so much physical strength, but moral and spiritual. Yet unlike Samson,

Paul had little hair! He belonged to the Elisha school of bald ministries from our understanding of historical reports and fresques. As an evangelist, this converted Pharisee was personally responsible for the spread of the Gospel throughout the whole of the Mediterranean northern coastline. What was his secret? Why did his preaching succeed?

Paul tells his secret to the Corinthians. 1 Corinthians 2:4 is so clear,

> "And my message and my preaching were not in persuasive words of wisdom, but in demonstration of the Spirit and of power."
>
> (NASB)

His preaching was marked by two spiritual qualities: a demonstration of the Holy Spirit and a demonstration of supernatural power. In the so called "Full Gospel" circles no distinction is usually made between them. We assume that it means that after we preach, we heal the sick, cast out demons, raise the dead and then counsel the thousands who have responded for salvation. Yet, Paul makes a clear distinction between Spirit and power and he isn't the only one. Luke makes the same distinction in speaking of Jesus' ministry:

> "You know of Jesus of Nazareth, how God anointed Him with the Holy Spirit and with power ... "
>
> (Acts 10:38 NASB)

Demonstrating power was an undeniable feature of Jesus' ministry and was carried on by early Church apostles and evangelists. The Gospel they preached was confirmed by the miracles they worked and to this day the power to heal the sick is a demonstrated reality when the Gospel is preached. However, there is one problem. In some geographical places this power was not able to be demonstrated, even by Jesus.

Mark 6:1–6 relates one of the most disappointing episodes in Jesus' ministry. By this time, He had proven that He had supernatural power available to Him. In the previous chapters He had stilled storms, delivered a demonically insane man, healed paralytics and raised a young girl from the dead. Nothing seems to be able to stand in His way until he visits His hometown Nazareth and there most of His power dries up. Mark sums it up in a single statement:

> "And He could do no miracle there except that He laid His hands on a few sick people and healed them."
>
> (Mark 6:5 NASB)

Think about this for a moment. The Son of God, filled with the Holy Spirit, anointed to perform works of power, sweeping all before Him everywhere, but in Nazareth He can't move in that power. The reason is given: unbelief. The people of Nazareth knew Joseph and Mary's boy too well and when you've known Jesus as a baby, it's hard to believe Him to be God.

## An evangelist in "Nazareth"

Towns and nations where unbelief is the air and people are breathing it, will experience a lack of supernatural power when the Gospel is preached. As an evangelist sent to France, I can certainly understand Jesus' Nazareth experience.

The French worldview has been largely influenced by the seventeenth-century philosopher and mathematician René Descartes who taught that the only way to arrive at truth is to doubt everything. His writings were in direct response to the imposition of religious dogma on society by the Church of the day who asserted that people had to believe certain things, no questions asked. The profound rejection of the domination of the Church on the thinking and the way of life of the French population was later to find its full expression in the French Revolution of 1789, the humanist philosophers of the nineteenth century, the student-led social revolution of May 1968, and the founding of the modern French secular state. Unbelief is now part of the very fabric of French society. Jesus is known, but only as a baby in a manger. This is Nazareth if ever there was one! As France ideologically weighs heavily on the whole of Europe, secular unbelief is an increasing reality that is not only present throughout the West, but is now also beginning to bite into Eastern Europe.

The implications for the preaching of the Gospel are enormous. As was the case in Nazareth, miracle power is stifled, even if a few sick people are still being healed through the laying on of hands. How charismatic Christians and ministries respond to this is vital for the future of the spread of the Gospel on this continent. Let's look at a number of the consequences.

Some charismatics refuse to acknowledge this reality and say any talk of limited power is unbelief itself. They adopt a "talk-it-up" approach. So a sick person healed is promoted as a mighty miracle. Western pagans are far from convinced however, when a Christian declares, "I feel better" after being prayed for. Others take the attention away from healing to put it on prophecy. Powerfully prophesying gives the speaker and the hearer the impression of supernatural power. But unsaved sceptics are, again, far from impressed. Please don't misunderstand me. I welcome the prophetic word and rejoice whenever an unwell Christian receives healing through prayer. However, I cannot build the legitimacy of the Gospel message on such occurrences. They are too unconvincing for the people I'm trying to win to Christ.

Fortunately, Jesus is still today, as yesterday, Jesus of Nazareth. He is successful in Nazareth and so can we be.

## God is in His words!

There is then, the other reason for Paul's effective Gospel preaching to the Corinthians: a demonstration of the Spirit. As we read further into 1 Corinthians 2, we find Paul talking about having the Holy Spirit in our words. When people, even unbelieving people, are exposed to a message presented with a demonstration of the Spirit, their hearts will be touched and they will say, "This man is not like the others." When God is in your words, the message penetrates through the unbelief and reaches the heart, drawing a favourable response.

After his mother was saved, Frederic, her eldest son, had to put up with her zeal for her new-found faith. Frederic was a rank unbeliever and a self-confessed Cartesian – a pure product of René Descartes. He was far from enthusiastic when his mother asked the whole family to attend a Sunday morning service where I was preaching. The following week Frederic's mother rang me to say that he had been touched by what he had heard. Some weeks later I was to do a private concert with my team in the family home for all the lady's friends. When he found out about it, Frederic cancelled his previous commitments and came along. I was stunned by his response. At the end of the evening, as people were leaving, he came to me with tears in his eyes saying, "I have been greatly affected by everything I've heard. Your words give me hope." No demonstration of power had occurred, but there had been a demonstration of the Spirit in the way the message was communicated.

This doesn't just happen. It is a deliberate attempt to use words and illustrations that won't feed the mind as much as touch the heart. Paul calls this, *"combining spiritual thoughts with spiritual words"* (1 Corinthians 2:13 NASB).

Reading back over the Nazareth narrative, we realise that if Jesus wasn't able to move in miracle power, He was nonetheless able to reach the people with His words. Unbelievers are surprised by the wisdom that flows when God is in the words. For this reason it was said of Him: *"for He was teaching them as one having authority, and not as their scribes"* (Matthew 7:29 NASB).

Therein lies the secret of an evangelist's success. Unlike Samson, his hair may be short, but his words must have spiritual authority and life for his unbelieving hearers. Many people love an opportunity to express their opinions. When we explain our knowledge to others, we take on the role of the superior party in any conversation or relationship. It feeds the pride in us. The hearer listens with more or less interest and is more or less impressed with the speaker's knowledge and his oratory skills, but his life is not changed. Whether the subject is religion, politics, culture, finance, sport or whatever, everyone loves to give his or her analysis. It's the norm in a world that talks, talks, talks. But when an evangelist speaks and God is in his words, faith is ignited and lives are changed forever. This is his secret.

## Ears that don't hear

There are many "sending" passages throughout the Bible, the two most well-known being Abram's call "to go forth" in Genesis 12:1 and Jesus' Great Commission to His disciples recorded in Mark 16:15. There is one, however, that we find in the Old Testament which has considerable importance for New Testament believers. Having just seen the Lord in all of His glory, the prophet Isaiah is cleansed of his unclean lips and hears God's call, *"Whom shall I send, and who will go for Us?"* (Isaiah 6:8 NASB). The prophet responds without hesitation, *"Here am I. Send me."* He is then given his instructions. He must go and speak to a people whose hearts are insensitive, whose ears are dull and whose eyes are dim. Because they have eyes that don't see, ears that don't hear and hearts that don't understand, they will not return to God and be healed and saved (Isaiah 6:9–10).

This same population is the target again and again in the New Testament. In fact, Jesus explains that He teaches in parables in order to separate those who see, hear and understand from those who don't. Literally quoting the above passage from Isaiah, Jesus speaks of salvation for those who have eyes that see and ears that hear (Matthew 13:13–16).

Significantly, this same passage of Isaiah appears in all four Gospels: Mark 4:11–12; Luke 8:10 and John 12:37–41, where Jesus laments that despite the many miracles they have seen, the Jews are still unbelieving. The reason for the unbelief is rooted in the Isaiah passage.

The unseeing eyes and unhearing ears of Isaiah 6 reappear in the Acts of the Apostles and again, significantly, in Paul's final recorded message to end Luke's documented history of the early Church, Acts 28:25–28. The impression we get is that this unbelieving people, present in the Old Testament as well as at the time of Jesus and in the first three decades of the early Church, would be a continuing obstacle that the evangelists of succeeding generations would have to confront.

In the light of this ongoing challenge we can understand why Jesus was sent to proclaim *"recovery of sight to the blind"* (Luke 4:18 NASB). Luke again quoting from Isaiah with obvious meaning beyond the physical realm.

Isn't it so true? People seem not to be able to grasp spiritual truth. It all sounds like a fairy tale to them. It reminds me of a door-knocking experience I once had whilst reaching out to the neighbours around our church in Ipswich, Australia. When the door opened, a pleasant middle-aged Asian lady appeared. She had a warm inviting smile so I began asking her the pastor-like questions one might ask when making contact with new people: "You have a lovely home, how long have you lived here?" She just kept smiling back. I thought this lady must be a shy person so I continued, "Do you have any children who may be interested in a youth group or children's club?" The smile never left her lips. "Boy, this is not easy," I thought. "Have you been able to get to know the neighbours?" still no vocal reply. "Excuse me, Madam, do you speak English?" It was only then that I realised that she was smiling back at me in Chinese. This lady hadn't understood a word. She could only hear my voice but could not understand my message. Spiritually, this is the case with most people in society and has been so since Old Testament days.

Paul explains that this is because *"the god of this world has blinded the minds of the unbelieving that they might not see the light of the gospel"* (2 Corinthians 4:4 NASB). Salvation comes when spiritual eyes are opened and light shines into human hearts. Evangelists are sent to accomplish this task.

## Opening blind eyes

The apostle Paul hears for every evangelist when Jesus speaks to him during his roadside conversion:

> *"... I am sending you, to open their eyes so that they may turn from darkness to light and from the dominion of Satan to God, that they may receive forgiveness of sins ..."*
> (Acts 26:17–18 NASB)

There it is. That's the evangelist's calling, to open eyes that don't see. In fact, salvation results from a confrontation between light and darkness – the light of the Holy Spirit in the evangelist overcoming the devil-imparted blindness that dwells within the unbeliever. John sums up successful evangelism perfectly in his first epistle: *"greater is He who is in you than he who is the world"* (1 John 4:4 NASB). It comes down to a spiritual confrontation between the Spirit that is in me and the spirit that is in him. Filled with the Holy Spirit and speaking words that pierce spiritual darkness, the evangelist has a winning advantage in this conflict. But God must be in the evangelist's words, otherwise eyes, ears and hearts will remain unseeing, unhearing and unfeeling.

It's the only explanation for Mr Ali's change of attitude, for example. My secretary was very surprised to receive a phone call from him one day, inviting me to do a concert in his central Paris piano/bar/restaurant. My CD album of French humorous Gospel songs hasn't reached number one on the hit parade yet, but it is opening some interesting doors.

Having received a copy of a promotional CD with extracts of my songs, Mr Ali was now inviting me to come to perform. But did he realise that it would be a pastor talking and singing about the love of God? I was not sure. His attitude was very business-like and rather unfriendly on the phone, explaining that he had a different group every night. He reluctantly agreed to provide a meal for four people, no more, and the rest we had to pay for. Five musicians and singers, plus my wife and my secretary makes seven, so I knew I was up for covering three meals. We arrived at the nightspot early to set up and when the boss came in, he didn't bother to greet me. We were doing our thing and he was doing his. Aren't people strange sometimes!

As the concert began, the place had filled up nicely and the air was full of cigarette smoke. After introducing myself and doing a first song, one couple got up and left to go to another room. You can't please everyone! Mr Ali was going about serving his customers as if we didn't exist, but someone did notice a smile as I dug deep trying to get the audience interested. As we pushed into the programme, the applause became more generous. It always seems to touch Frenchmen when you talk about love, so I carefully set the scene before singing my love song to Denise, my wife. "Guys, have you found the woman of your dreams?" Sometimes they reply, "Yeah, ten of them!" "I have," I continued, "and I've been living with her for over twenty-five years." Someone called out, "You're a lucky man!" Young people today celebrate their silver anniversary after twenty-five days!

"This is my song, dedicated to the one who has shared twenty-five years of my life." The ladies were moved with emotion and the men didn't know what to think. The song says, "Denise, tell me your secret." Her secret, of course, is her love for God. By the time I had finished, there was a sentimental hush in the place. It was now the moment to reach into their hearts. I sang my testimony song, "When I gaze up into the heavens." Cigarette haze had been replaced by the presence of God and no one moved. At the end of the night, as we were packing away the gear, I went to see Mr Ali standing behind his bar. "I've come to pay for the three meals I owe you," I said. He shook my hand and gave me a rare smile, "There's nothing to pay, it's all on the house. When can you come back again?"

Hey, these Parisians aren't that tough after all! So John says, "Greater is He that is in me than he that is in the world." It was certainly true that night in Mr Ali's piano-bar.

# Getting People to Listen ... and to Respond

We have seen how the literal meaning of the Greek word translated "evangelist" in the New Testament is "one who announces good news" and that for news to be "good" for the hearer, it must be perceived by him as something that will enrich him personally. Ultimately, people always ask the question, "What's in it for me?" However, a good news message must not only be perceived as good news, it must be well-communicated. If communication is poor, it will invariably lead to confusion and uncertainty.

Paris has an amazing public transport system. Anyone who has travelled on the underground, called the Metro, has seen the efficient way it operates. There is also what is called the RER network. Commuters on these trains are brought rapidly in and out of the city from the suburbs. This also runs efficiently – except for the public address system. When they try to announce problems that have occurred on the line, it's difficult to grasp what has happened and what a passenger must do. You just hear the odd word like, "Closed ... (crackle) ... change ... (crackle) ... get off ... (crackle)." It's hard to work out what to do and that is particularly worrying!

To avoid taking the car to the airport to catch a plane, I decided to make my way to the Charles De Gaulle airport using the RER train. All was well until a message came across the public address system. "Closed ... (crackle) ... get off ... (crackle) ... bus ... (crackle) ... airport (crackle) ..." Confusion fell on everyone in the carriage. We all realised that the train wouldn't take us the airport and that buses would be used to get us to the terminals, but no one seemed sure at which station to get off to catch the bus. I had an idea and so when we stopped at the station I thought was the right one, I got off. The railway agent didn't seem to know what I was talking about when I asked him about the buses to the airport. "In any case, it's not here," he said. "Try the next station." So I had to wait for the following train, feeling my blood pressure rising to dangerous levels. After all, I had a plane to catch and if you arrive late they call you a "no-show". A train finally came and getting off at the next station, I eventually found a bus that took me to the airport. As I always allow plenty of time in order to deal with unforeseen problems, I did get to Charles De Gaulle in time to catch my plane, but I certainly could have done without the stress.

I nearly missed my plane for one reason – poor communication. The message was good and one I needed to hear, but communication was bad.

## TV ads, don't you love them?

To draw the right response from people, a message must be presented in a way that is simple, clear and interesting to the person for whom it is intended.

Advertising agencies can be of great help in this area. They have literally made the response of the consumer the centre of their attention. Every ad is carefully prepared to have an impact and as evangelists, we would be well advised to learn from them as we are in the same business of drawing a response from people. Television advertising has become so creative that a twenty-four-hour channel devoted exclusively to advertisements has been launched in the UK and on other stations programmes are regularly aired showing the world's best TV ads. The success of an advertising campaign will have a significant effect on sales of a particular product and of course, this is the desired end result. Poor advertising will conversely have a negative effect on the image of the brand.

Australian males have traditionally loved their beer. So Australian brewers compete for a big market and advertise accordingly. Perhaps one of the very best ads I've seen was for the Queensland brewers Castlemaine Perkins whose beer is called XXXX. Keep in mind that the target group is macho Aussie males.

The scene opens with a pretty girl in pigtails who looks a little like Barbie. She has a frog in one hand and a dream in her heart.

She would so dearly love to turn the frog into a handsome young prince. So, predictably, she kisses the frog and her dream comes true. The frog turns into a tall, square-chinned, big-chested male, dressed in a blue singlet and a bushman's hat – the kind of specimen you would find in any iron man's race on an Australian beach. She is so happy and reaches up on her toes to kiss her man. When the second kiss takes place, instantly, the girl turns into a chilled can of XXXX beer. Now it's the man's dream that has come true! He drinks the can with obvious pleasure and when he has finished, he looks at it intently and says to the can, "Hey, you wouldn't have a sister, would you?"

The message may not be very good, but the way it was presented was great! If then, a poor message can be well communicated, so also can a good message be poorly communicated.

An evangelist must learn to become a good communicator. Some are born with an outstanding speaking gift, but communication is ultimately an acquired skill. As you improve your ability to communicate with the general public, you will be surprised and thrilled at how much they enjoy you and how much you enjoy them.

## Get smart, Maxwell

One of the stories I tell on the streets that the crowds like best is entitled, "Do you speak English?" Now, this story is told with a sketchboard on the streets of Paris and plays on the inadequacy many French people feel when it comes to expressing themselves in English. I tell the story of a young man from London who arrives in Paris. His name is MAXWELL and the reason he comes to Paris is that he wants to have FUN. To appeal to Parisian girls he wants to appear COOL. So he has to work on his LOOK. The words in capital letters that appear on the board are understood by the French, though sometimes with different shades of meaning to common English usage. The story continues: Maxwell discovers that life in Paris is expensive so he has to find a JOB. But he has ambition, so he looks for something at the TOP. To land a good job he wants to be seen as having plenty of PUNCH, so everything he does, he does with SPEED. By now the crowd is enthralled and it builds ... However, Maxwell discovers that life in Paris is HARD and for all his hopes and effort, it's all a bit of a FLOP, so he ends up experiencing the BLUES. But the story will have a HAPPY ENDING. A friend of Maxwell arrives in Paris and finds him in a sorry state, so he has two pieces of advice to give. The first is: RELAX MAX, but it's the second one that changes everything for Maxwell: Max, GOD LOVES YOU. You see Max, you've launched out in life with many hopes and expectations, but things haven't turned out that way. You've forgotten about the One who can guide you through life. Now, if you place yourself in the hands of a loving God, His good plan will come about in your life.

The university students enjoy Maxwell and professors have even been heard discussing among themselves about the possibility of my coming to give a lecture on communication, such is their surprise to see the way their students listen and respond to me. But we all know, everyone loves a good story. Apparently, nothing much has changed since the days of Jesus' parables.

## Becoming a good preacher

The Gospel is a message that must be preached and preached well. Good Gospel preaching is what Paul is talking about in the important passage of 1 Corinthians 9:20–22. The Apostle's goal is clearly to win Jews, those under the law, those without the law, and the weak as well. He is looking for response and genuine conversions to Christ. The means to that end is the ability to communicate to these different people groups in the way each understands. It's so obvious, really. To win someone you first have to reach him or her in a meaningful way. In fact, the definition for successful evangelism is found in these verses:

> "I have become all things to all men, so that I may by all means save some."
>
> (1 Corinthians 9:22 NASB)

Reaching a person means understanding how he or she thinks and feels and speaking into their life in a way they appreciate. It's getting inside their skin, their head and heart, to leave a lasting impression. If, as I suggest, the Gospel is not an explanation but an invitation, then Gospel preaching is not speaking at people but bringing the hearers into an experience which you, as the speaker, will experience with them. Gospel preaching must make people laugh, cry, react, feel warmth and tenderness as well as indignation and conviction. As they hear preaching that moves them, a response is already taking place well before any altar call for salvation is given.

## Features of a boring sermon

There is nothing more painful to endure than a boring sermon. As kids, we would go to church each Sunday at the local parish church. The minister was a fine man, dedicated to God and people but, sadly for all of us, he was a poor preacher. Each Sunday for twenty minutes he would torture himself and us with highly forgettable sermons. It has led me to the view that the Church is the only institution in society that has the power to get people out of a comfortable bed on a Sunday morning only to put them back to sleep on a hard bench and get them to pay for it.

I've heard thousands of sermons in my time. Some have been great and life-changing. Many were, dare I say it, a waste of time. I have come to the view that just because the speaker claims to be filled with the Holy Spirit, we, as hearers, are not necessarily guaranteed a good sermon. Communicating the Gospel well also requires us to understand how not to communicate it!

You know it's a boring sermon when:

- Fifteen minutes into it you are still not sure what it's about.
- There's a procession of abstract ideas and beautiful words with little practical importance to you. An example of this can be found in the plaque that hung on a pastor's wall bearing the title, "What is the Anointing?" The definition given was: "The overflowing of the Messiah's divine life of holiness into a human life which has been consecrated to God through personal cross experience which makes it spiritually rich and able to impart effectively the light and fragrance of God's Word into the lives of others, producing

in them deep spiritual satisfaction and obvious Christian fruitfulness." Did you get all that? Personally, I love God's anointing, but that plaque doesn't help me much.
- The sermon is a succession of exhortations and directives: to do or not to do, or as someone once said, "Woulda, coulda, shoulda."
- The key statements pass unnoticed.
- The voice is without conviction, as flat as the highway stretching endlessly through Australia's Nullabor Desert.
- You feel sorry for the speaker and for yourself for being there.
- You hit your watch during the sermon, thinking it has broken down.
- You find yourself counting the bricks in the wall behind the preacher.
- You find yourself thinking about lunch and whether you'll go to a Chinese, Greek or Italian restaurant.
- You have that terrible feeling of not knowing when he will stop and a fear that the speaker doesn't know when he will stop either.
- You say "Amen", not because you necessarily agree, but because you hope he gets the message.
- You find it hard to look him in the eye at the end of service.

The truth of the matter is that the power of the Word will only be experienced if the preacher is powerful.

## The interest factor

To win a person you must firstly reach him or her and to do that you must be interesting. Interest is the only thing that will turn a hearer into a listener. All preachers need to understand that they have in front of them people who, for years, have been programmed by television-watching. Colour television is an amazing visual experience. Sets are lavish and the action is spectacular and fast moving, supported by music appropriate for every mood. Viewers are conditioned to be continually grabbed by something interesting.

If the interest begins to fail what does the viewer do? Does he turn off the TV? Of course not! He reaches for the remote control and zaps. When I'm on the streets and the interest level of what I'm saying dips, people leave. In church, when the preacher stops being interesting, Christians are more polite! They don't get up and leave, but they do reach for the mental remote control and zap onto something more interesting: problems at work, the next holiday, the big game on TV tonight.

We have several advantages over the TV as preachers. Firstly, we preach a fantastic message that relates to everyone's life. Then, we have at our disposal the anointing of the Holy Spirit which must be channelled into our preaching and of course, we are real and not virtual. But, despite all of this we still need to be interesting!

Ray was a typical Aussie who loved life; a nice guy but not too tuned into God. He came one Sunday night to a special visitors' service we were having in the church, but not really because he was searching for answers for his life. His primary goal in coming was to get his sister off his back. He seemed however, to really enjoy himself and surprisingly, the following Sunday he was back. When I spoke with him at the end of the service, he told me that what he particularly liked were the humorous stories I told. Then he said this: "I'm finding church more interesting than the Sunday night movie on TV." Isn't that an interesting comment! The first few times Ray came for the stories, but it wasn't long before the Word, that double-edged sword, pierced his heart and he was wonderfully saved. Several years later he began training for the ministry and today he preaches the Gospel, trying as he might to be more interesting than the Sunday night movie.

## Features of an effective evangelistic sermon

Now that we are determined not to preach boring sermons, let's look at what touches hearers in our preaching:

### 1. The human warmth of the speaker
People rarely respond to a speaker whom they don't like and don't trust. A music teacher once put it this way: "If my pupil doesn't love me he will learn nothing from me." A hearer who hears a speaker for the first time will very quickly make up his mind if he can relate to him or not. Being yourself and being real in front of a crowd creates trust that allows response.

### 2. The intensity of the speaker's personal convictions
When Peter spoke out boldly before the council of the Jews in Jerusalem, the impact on those religious leaders came not from the content of the defence, but from the confidence that they observed in Peter and John (Acts 4:13). They had the same authority that Jesus showed.

Many incidents have confirmed to me the importance of

personal convictions being communicated to the hearers. A couple came one Sunday and found Christ in our church in Australia. There was nothing very sophisticated about them; the kind of folk where what you see is what you get. After a few months in the church, one day in a conversation with them they made a surprising statement to me. "Vince, do you know what it is we like best in your sermons? When you get mad and you bang your fist on the pulpit, it stirs us." I don't make a practice of destroying pulpits, especially after wrecking one in full flight in Marseille, France some years ago. However, I did take note of what they were expressing to me. They liked conviction from the speaker.

I will never forget a sermon preached by a Korean pastor called Billy Kim at the Billy Graham Congress for world evangelists in Amsterdam in Holland in 1986. His subject was "Evangelists and Revival" and he told the 8,000 delegates the reason Korea had experienced revival during the twentieth century. He spoke about the suffering of the Korean Christians at the hands of the Japanese, because of their faith. As he preached through his own tears, 8,000 evangelists wept with him.

Isn't it this that comes through in Paul's words to the Romans,

> "I have great sorrow and unceasing grief in my heart. For I could wish that I myself were accursed, separated from Christ for the sake of my brethren, my kinsmen according to the flesh."
>
> (Romans 9:2–3 NASB)

It is indeed very true that fire ignites fires.

### 3. Subjects that everyone can relate to

If people are to listen to a speaker they must find him or her relevant. In the hearer's mind pops a question, "Are they talking about my life?" In Western society there are two charges levelled against the Church. Firstly, there is the problem of hypocrisy. So often church people have not lived according to the values they hold. The other serious reproach is that the Church has lost touch. It doesn't understand people and their needs. There will never be a response if the message is not relevant. So we preach not about faith, but about how a person can have faith; not so much about who God is, but how a person can know God. This is where evangelists differ from teachers in their approach to preaching. They seek a response.

### 4. Telling a good story

One of the best ways to gauge if you are an interesting speaker is to observe how attentive the children are in the meeting. A simple rule is: If you keep the children's interest, you'll keep the adults tuned in. But if you lose the kids, it won't be long before the adults wander off in their thoughts.

People of all ages love a good story and it was because He was a great storyteller that Jesus was a master communicator. It will be an evangelist's storytelling that will allow him not only to maintain interest, but especially to plant truth into the imaginations and memory banks of his hearers. Something that has always pleased me is that, years after hearing a sermon, people come up and remind me about a story I told that they have never forgotten. They may not remember the Scripture that I read, but they got the message from the picture I painted in their imagination.

Of the many stories I tell, the one that I saw make the greatest impact was about a toad. It was about the way in which God began to deal with me about having compassion for unlovely people. Cane toads in Queensland are a real pest. They were introduced into the cane fields to kill off the dangerous snakes, but have become a major ecological problem in their own right. They come out especially in the rainy season and sit in their hundreds on the road. Motorists have no pangs of conscience about running right over them and when one is flattened you do feel a slight thump on the tyres. It's hard to believe that God actually created them because they are just so ugly!

One day, as I was making my way down the garden to the car, I saw one of these big toads on my front lawn. Without hesitating, I gave it a good kick and this toad, which normally doesn't fly, became airborne and landing on my wire fence became caught in it. Getting into the car I thought to myself, "Serves him right!" But as I was driving away, I heard this word ringing in my mind, "murderer". It came strongly enough for me to stop the car, turn around and return home. Before long I had freed the toad and was off again with a clear conscience. The following day however, walking past the fence, I noticed the flying toad on the grass. It was dead and I felt really bad about myself and my attitude towards unlovely things.

I told this story in an evangelistic service one Sunday night. In the service was a man, present for the first time and a rank unbeliever. He was not one of those who responded to the altar call to come to Christ that night. However, in the week that followed he went fishing with some friends in a boat. They were not alone. Some pelicans were also there, paddling around doing their own spot of fishing. At one stage the man who had been present in the service on Sunday, threw out his line which passed over one of the pelicans. When the bird felt the line he panicked and got entangled in it. The unfeeling friends had a simple solution, "Cut the line", they said. It was then that the cane toad story flashed back into his mind. He too would be a hard-hearted murderer! Despite the protests of the others, he insisted on rowing over to the pelican and setting it free. The following Sunday night that man was back in church. His heart, now free from the hardness he had known, was ready and when the appeal was made he gave his life to Christ.

Life is full of striking stories that touch us and make us think. If they are well told, they become powerful tools for the Holy Spirit to draw responses to the Gospel message.

## Building a good salvation altar call

Making a public call for unsaved people to come to Christ is profoundly biblical. In fact, Jesus did it all the time. "Come, follow Me", was His approach and He did not hesitate to call for a public response. Zacchaeus coming down from the tree was hardly an intimate private moment between him and Jesus. In fact, public response is essential to salvation. Jesus made this very challenging statement:

> "Therefore, whoever confesses Me before men, him I will also confess before My Father who is in heaven."
>
> (Matthew 10:32 NKJV)

Here are some simple instructions:

1. The call for response begins at the very moment the evangelist comes to the microphone. Everything he says and does is a preparation for a response by his hearers at the altar call.
2. Whatever the specific theme of the sermon, a word, a thought or a verse of Scripture will be the launching pad to building the altar invitation. A hearer who attends meetings regularly will clearly know when the evangelist moves into altar call mode. There is a clear sense of changing up gears.
3. The tone of the appeal must never be hard. The voice will need to be gentle but insistent, searching people's hearts.
4. It must never be rushed. Responding to the Gospel publicly is a daunting prospect for most people, even if they sincerely wish to do it. Give it time and build confidence.
5. The evangelist needs to emphasise that the invitation is for people who have never before made a commitment to Christ. Congregations lose confidence in evangelists when they see most of the response coming from insecure Christians. The evangelist rejoices thinking it's a response for salvation, but the congregation is not fooled. The angels in heaven rejoice over one sinner who comes to repentance, not over ten Christians who want to come forward again and again.
6. We can fully expect people who respond to salvation altar calls to be emotionally touched. When tears flow as a person responds to the Gospel, it may be in remorse over his or her sins but, more likely in this era where consciousness of sin is

at an all time low, tears will come as the person feels the love and presence of God touching their life and healing hurts. There's something very special about a person crying in the presence of God and even more so when it's a man!
7. The practical methods for conducting the appeal will vary according to the situation and the preferences of each evangelist. Where possible a suitable chorus needs to be decided on with the musicians and song leader prior to the meeting. Anointed music from the time of David and Elisha has always been an important setting for the work of the Holy Spirit in human hearts.

In our church in Paris many have been saved standing out the front at the end of the meeting on the same floor tile. It has almost become a sacred spot! Often people refer to it with a smile on their face, "I was saved on that floor tile." The tile, of course, is of no importance, but it serves as a reminder that one day you publicly responded to the Gospel and gave your life to Christ in that place. It's like the memorial stones of the Old Testament. May every church have a sacred floor tile or square metre of carpet where people respond to the most beautiful message that has ever been preached.

# 5

# *Being Well Received*

There is so much to learn from Luke 10:5–12 about being an evangelist and how to be effective. Jesus is sending out seventy evangelists (what an outreach!) and He is giving them His final instructions. He talks about prayer and how one is sent out, what not to take and how not to be distracted from the mission. However most of Jesus' final instructions have to do with how an evangelist is to be received.

This is absolutely vital. The way an evangelist is received will ultimately determine his success. Jesus Himself was only able to exercise His ministry when He was well received. He had been welcomed by the Galileans, so it was in Capernaum that He set up His base and primarily operated His ministry (John 4:45). At

Nazareth Jesus was not honoured as a man sent from heaven, so His ministry was very limited (Matthew 13:53–58). When He tried to enter a Samaritan town, Jesus was not well received and He was not able to minister there (Luke 9:52–53). However, years later there was a radical change in the attitude of the Samaritans. When they received Philip the evangelist and the Gospel he preached, great revival broke out. Acts 8:14 gives us the reason for the revival: Samaria had received the Word of God. This word "received" seems to have great significance in the success of an evangelistic ministry.

## There's blessing in receiving

The Greek word translated "to receive" is rich in meaning and nuance. It is the word *dekomai* which does not have the sense of "taking" but rather "welcoming what is arriving". Whatever your favourite sport, perhaps one of the greatest of human sporting struggles is played out on a rugby field. All rugby players know that to receive a pass you have to let the ball come to you and pouch it in your hands and arms. If you snatch at the ball you are likely to drop it and spoil the advance of the team. The receiving of a pass is very much the sense of the Greek word *dekomai*.

This word had three specific meanings to the New Testament Greek reader:

1. *Acceptance – reception.* This referred to receiving gifts, payments, parcels, or goods sent. The word was also used when God accepted a person's sacrifice or when someone accepted the circumstances of his life. A host would open

his door and receive a visitor. Heaven would "receive" a deceased Christian.
2. **Understand**. Someone willing to understand truth would "receive" it and want to learn about it. When someone received truth he would acknowledge it as such. Being touched by a testimony is receiving it in one's heart. It is also accepting the Word of God and understanding it as the truth that sets us free (John 8:32).
3. **To honour**. To acknowledge someone or something as he or it truly is. It is opening one's heart to another person just as the Corinthians opened their hearts to Titus because he was sent by Paul (2 Corinthians 7:13–15). Honour also involves pleasing someone. But let us go further in understanding the principle of honouring an evangelist.

## The principle of being honoured

Matthew 10:40 has great consequences for the evangelist. In this passage Jesus makes the statement, *"He who receives you receives Me, and he who receives Me receives Him who sent Me"* (NASB). Welcoming God requires of a person that he welcomes the one bringing the message of God. The apostle Paul expressed the same thought in an amazing declaration when he wrote to the Galatians about the way they had initially welcomed him: *"... but you received me as an angel of God, as Christ-Jesus Himself"* (Galatians 4:14 NASB). Think about it for a moment. Those who welcome us and open themselves up to us, as evangelists, are opening up to Jesus Himself. Wow! We become angels or messengers of God to other people. In fact, as receiving the emissary is receiving the

One who sent him, so receiving an evangelist is a clear expression of opening up to God. This has real implications for where an evangelistic ministry should operate.

When on the streets, I often find myself speaking with young people. At the end of the conversation I say to them, "Thank you for respecting me. Others don't respect me as a pastor but you do because you respect God. You don't mock God and He sees that and He will touch you and bless you because you respect Him." Invariably the young people reply to these statements by saying *merci* (thank you).

As a pastor, I have been exposed to different reactions from the neighbours we have never chosen to have. Some are impressed, others are indifferent and others again are frankly hostile. In one suburb of Paris where we lived, our neighbours were rather hostile to a pastor. Those living opposite us spoke with irony and obviously mocked God and indirectly mocked us for representing Him. Those who lived behind us had no respect for anyone. When the parents were away on holidays the son and daughter brought in their friends and partied all night nearly every night. Refusing to listen to our pleas for some quiet, I finally called the police at 2.00am. The music did go down a notch but the revellers went out into the garden and cried out with derision, "Hallelujah. This pastor is not very merciful!" Denise and I were very pleased to sell up and leave these disrespectful people.

Our new neighbours were so different. Across the road was a couple who were traditionalist Catholics preferring Latin to French for their liturgy. "I am so pleased to have a man of God as a neighbour," said the man. Once, when needing to be operated on for a throat infection, the surgeon said to me as I was pulling out my cheque book, "I never charge a man of prayer for my services." How surprising! This also occurred one time when I visited an optometrist to order reading glasses. The way they received me as a pastor is a reflection of the way they receive God.

Receiving a man of God always precedes a visitation of God. When the Galatians welcomed the apostle Paul as "an angel of God" they experienced spiritual revival. The vital lesson to be learnt from this principle is that the success of evangelism is directly linked to the way an evangelist is welcomed and received.

## Testing the welcome

Let's go back to Luke 10:5. Jesus speaks of an evangelistic strategy that seeks to enter the houses of unsaved people. If doors literally open, hearts have opened and the Gospel can take root.

The principle of Luke 10:5 can be summarised in the following way:

- Enter into a house, or in other words, attempt to get on a personal basis with a person.
- Give out the peace that is in you.
- If it finds a "child of peace" the spiritual life that is in you rests on him.
- If there is no "child of peace" your spiritual life will return to you and you will be unable to share your faith.

One of the more reactionary university campuses in France is at Jussieu in Paris. Yet, surprisingly things happen even among the reputedly anarchic student population. One Friday afternoon in front of a sizeable crowd, a young woman listened in with obvious scepticism. However, while I was speaking I could visibly see a transformation taking place on her face. From a totally closed look, I saw openness and then a radiant smile. At the end of my sketchboard message Chantal, my secretary and zealous evangelist in her own right, spoke with her. "As that man was speaking," said the perplexed onlooker, "I felt a peace overwhelm me." Yet, the environment was anything but peaceful. In fact, I had to contend that day with an extremely loud group of Brazilian percussionists and dancers nearby and my voice projection was more that of a fish seller at a market than the soft tones one usually associates with Jesus talking to an individual. However, somehow the peace that is in me found a child of peace in that lady and that peace settled on her.

## Noah's dove

A very interesting parallel could be drawn between looking for a "child of peace" and Noah sending out his dove to see when the flood had come to an end. After floating endlessly on flood waters for many days, Noah sends out the dove, which itself is a symbol of peace, to see if the waters are abating. However, the dove finds no place where it can settle and so returns to the ark. Noah waits another seven days. He sends out the dove a second time seeking dry land and a place of rest. Again, the dove returns but this time with an olive leaf in its beak. That's a very positive sign, but it is still not the final answer. A further seven days elapse. For a third time Noah releases the dove, which by now is really confused about what is happening. This time the dove does not return. It has found a resting place.

There is a beautiful parallel to be drawn here for evangelists. As evangelists we send out our peace looking for a "child of peace" on whom it will rest. Not finding one, it returns to us. We send it out a second time and while again it returns to us, it does have a leaf in its beak. There's something out there. Out goes the peace a third time, but this time it's different. It doesn't return to us. It has found a child of peace on whom to settle. Our Gospel of peace has found a home in a human heart. Somebody is responding to us and responding to God.

At the Jussieu campus I am continually sending out my dove looking for a child of peace. One day at the end of a sketchboard message a number of people came forward and took my brochure. The first to move was a tall young man in a soccer jersey from the well-known Marseille club. He took my piece of literature and quickly disappeared. Not even one half-hour later he was back wanting to talk with me. His question was one I have often heard, "How can you be sure that God really exists?" I replied boldly, "You do not know if He exists, but at this very moment He's drawing you to Himself" "How you mean?" he blurted out with astonishment. "Well, firstly," I said, "you did not leave mocking me when I spoke about God. You showed great respect for Him and secondly, you have returned to talk with me personally about God." "It's true! it's true!" he chanted, as light hit his darkened mind.

That same day another incident occurred. A whole band of young people stopped to listen to me and as I finished one said to me, "Can I write something on your board?" I said, "Okay, as long as it is not rude." So he and a friend began to draw graffiti of a good level. To one of them I said, "What's your name?" "Stephane," he replied. So I said, "Well, Stephane, you have just put the yellow paintbrush in the blue pot of paint. "Oh," he said "I'm very sorry." So now with the initiative, I said to him, "Stephane, I would like to pray for you." "Thank you, sir," he said with genuine sincerity. "What would you like me to pray for you for?" I continued. He said, "For my baccalaureate. Please pray that I will pass my exams." "Okay," I said, "I will, but after getting your 'bac' I want to see you at church, Stephane." "Oh yes, sir," he said again with great sincerity. Well, I never did see him at church, but I know that my peace sent forth had settled on a child of peace that day.

## Cities and towns

The Luke 10 passage speaks of individual homes, but in the Matthew 10 version of these same instructions Jesus gives us another dimension still. Verse 11 speaks of towns and villages and the child of peace has a different name: "he who is worthy (of receiving you)". Such a man is worthy of you, of your peace and of your God. This man is the key to evangelising his city and he is the key to the success of your evangelistic strategy.

One area within greater Paris has so clearly illustrated this principle. It is the town of Saint Germain-en-Laye and it began when a lady working at the Council Chambers was saved and took up the burden for the town. Shortly after, my peace fell on the owner of a well-known café-brasserie in the centre of town. He eagerly invited me to run a Bible study in his café on a fortnightly basis. Then a Chinese lady who had been saved through my sketchboard evangelism and who was living in that same area began to gather Asian women in the area for another Bible study group. But the openings didn't stop there. The local Protestant reformed church pastor who had initially given me a rather frosty reception attended some of my Bible studies and promptly offered me the use of all his facilities. He also invited me to preach in his parish church, which I did with much gratitude to him and to God. The ball continued to roll. Next was a lady of German descent who was saved through the café Bible Study. Having reached retirement age, she was alarmed at the number of years of her life she had wasted and wanted to make up for lost time. Her large lounge room is now serving the cause of the Kingdom of God. Twice we have conducted private concerts in her home to a packed audience of around forty people, friends and neighbours, most of whom were unsaved. Bible studies in her home followed together with a children's club on a Saturday afternoon for the kids in the area. One lady became the key to the town and region, showing herself "worthy" of receiving an evangelist.

Jesus' way to evangelise is to penetrate into homes and towns. We have some wonderful examples in the New Testament of encounters with people on whom the dove of peace settled and who became key people for the salvation of others.

There was Jesus and Levi in Luke 5:27–32. Having responded to the call that Jesus had placed on his life, Levi became the door to a whole group of people who gravitated around him. He arranged a dinner in his home for all his friends so that they might meet and hear Jesus. I personally believe that it was his experience at Levi's home around the meal that led to Jesus' instructions to his seventy evangelists in Luke 10.

Then there was the meeting between Jesus and Zacchaeus. Jesus invited Himself to stay at his home that day. When Zacchaeus received Him into his home, salvation entered into his whole household. This man, as fathers were in those days, was the key to his family and as a child of peace, became the doorway for reaching and winning all those associated with him. In John's Gospel we also have the example of the nameless woman at the well who was the child of peace for the Samaritan town of Sychar. Because of the way she responded to Jesus, a whole town was saved.

There were other exciting encounters that led to the salvation of many. When Peter met Cornelius, the dove of peace landed on the child of peace. Cornelius, the Roman centurion, honoured Peter as a man of God and gathered his household to hear him. This included children but also slaves and all those who came under his authority. We can imagine that there were present at that meeting other high-ranking officers based at Caesarea. Cornelius was the key person. Because Cornelius welcomed Peter, the Holy Spirit fell on them all.

Lydia was also a child of peace on whom the dove landed. This lady had a reverential fear of God and when Paul spoke, she listened to him with an open heart. This is always a winning formula. A child of peace will always reveal himself or herself by showing a profound respect for God and an attentive desire to hear God's Word. Lydia had a spiritual experience as she listened to Paul. God opened her heart.

When Lydia was saved she asked Paul and his team to stay at her home. I really feel that Paul missed a wonderful occasion here. Wouldn't Lydia have made a perfect wife for him and what a beautiful love story that would have made! I suppose however, you couldn't expect any woman to be able to put up with the apostle Paul.

One day as I was presenting a sketchboard message, I was aware of a fine looking man listening to me intently. As I finished, he approached me and made a surprising statement. He said to me, "I see light in your eyes." "And I see tears in yours," I replied. The following day he was in church and at the altar call came forward to make a commitment to Christ. Once again, as in the Bible accounts, the dove had found a resting place.

## Recapping how to recognise a child of peace

In summary, these are the signs that you have found a child of peace who is likely to be receptive to the Gospel message:

1. Respect for a man of God
2. Listening attentively to the Word
3. Asking personal questions
4. The desire to meet again
5. The desire to speak again about faith
6. The desire to come to a meeting
7. The desire to have other acquaintances hear about faith

## Getting practical

A person with genuine spiritual sensitivity will receive a man of God. The welcome given by that person will allow the evangelist to enter into his or her home.

Evangelism in houses usually happens at the dining table. This is a most enjoyable way to evangelise, but you have to be careful not to put on too much weight! How do you get invited to dinner? Simple, invite them over to your house first!

An evangelist can also enter a person's home as a "doctor" (Luke 5:31). Jesus found Himself in the midst of publicans healing their troubled lives. When someone experiences difficulties or goes through a crisis, he is more ready to open up his home to welcome the one who will bring him comfort and support.

An evangelist may also have access to a person's home to give practical help. This can come in the form of repairs in the home of a single woman, providing transport for the one who has none or even providing a meal for one who has trouble cooking for himself. Bearing gifts is another way an evangelist can penetrate into a home. This may be for someone moving into the area or for a new-born baby or for Christmas.

Surprisingly, many will welcome you into their home simply to pray with them. In one particular area of Paris we distributed envelopes in letter boxes inviting people to make known to us their personal prayer requests. For a period of several months, every day we received in the mail one, two or even three requests for prayer for particular needs from people we didn't know. The intimate details written on the returned prayer slips showed us to what extent people would allow us into their personal lives for the purpose of prayer. Praying for needs is one thing that no other agency or body in society can offer to hurting people.

As evangelists, we each have a dove of peace to release. Where it lands will reveal a door that opens for reaching whole families, villages or people groups. Let's release those doves and see where they land!

# PART TWO

## *The Good Samaritan*

# Why Did Jesus Choose a Samaritan as the Hero of His Story?

Who doesn't know the story of the Good Samaritan told by Jesus in Luke's Gospel (Luke 10:30–37)? Even people who have never read the Bible seem to have heard about it and know that it has to do with someone doing a good turn to a person who had a problem. When Parisians hear the term they immediately think of the major department store bearing the name of Samaritan on the famous Rue de Rivoli in the shopping heart of Paris. The story of the Good Samaritan is not a true story! It's a parable created by Jesus to convey an important spiritual lesson. If we go back to the beginning of the conversation that inspired it, we discover that the story comes as a second phase answer to that question, "What do I have to do to go to heaven?" so the answer is important. The details of the narrative are of vital significance as Jesus has specifically included them.

The victim of the attack by the robbers has been beaten, robbed and left half dead. It immediately brings to mind what Jesus said of the work of the devil as a thief who *"comes only to steal and kill and destroy"* (John 10:10 NASB). In this parable we have an amazing spiritual parallel of a lost soul destined to die and the evangelist coming to rescue him and restore him to life.

Though the parable can be interpreted in terms of social action to help those in physical need, it is totally consistent with Scripture to give it a spiritual interpretation, all the more so because Jesus is still answering the question, "What must I do to inherit eternal life?"

Let's face it, Jesus just didn't like the religious leaders of His day. Both the priest and the Levite in the parable had perfect doctrine. In fact, if both passed over to the other side, it wasn't because they were pretending they hadn't seen the poor fellow. To totally abide by the religious laws, they couldn't run the risk of touching a corpse and making themselves unclean. However, it's a pretty sad day when your religion makes you pass on the other side of someone in need, even if it is a strict application of Old Testament Scripture.

Jesus is at His provocative best when He makes a Samaritan His knight in shining armour, coming to the rescue. Jews and

Samaritans hated each other and were not even on speaking terms. That's what the woman at the well said to Jesus. And if the attack happened on the road between Jerusalem and Jericho, this was inside Israel's territory. The victim would most probably have been a Jew. The priest and Levite didn't want to get involved, but the Samaritan is not bothered about cultural and social conflicts so he steps in.

## Where is love?

Think about it. The religious leaders and teachers of God's revealed Word did nothing for a suffering person, but the Samaritan's religion could not allow him to walk past.

Now, there's a real problem here. His religion didn't enjoy all the revealed truth that Judaism possessed. As a matter of fact, Samaritan religion was based only on the Pentateuch, the first five books of the Old Testament. They had the law but not the prophets.

It's hard to believe that Jesus would deliberately promote someone whose doctrine wasn't totally right. Yet, that is exactly what happened. And what is even worse, is the inference that the Samaritan would inherit eternal life while the priest and Levite would not!

How offensive this is to us as evangelical Christians. We have the truth of the Gospel. I am firmly convinced that evangelical interpretation of the Bible is the right way to understand God's Word. Yet, the parable of the Good Samaritan shows us that we can have God's truth without God's love for the lost. And ultimately it's love that wins Jesus' commendation. It is disturbing in the same way as Matthew 7:21–23 is to charismatic ministers: how can you prophesy, cast out demons and perform miracles all in Jesus' name and miss out on heaven? Apparently, it is possible!

This must make the cold, unfeeling and judgmental evangelical rethink how he is living out his faith. His ability to explain God's plan of redemption from the Garden of Eden to the throne room of heaven is simply not enough to win God's approval. His heart must respond to hurting people.

But there's more!

In recent years, in charismatic circles, so much has been made of prophecy, and prophets have been in big demand. Of course, prophecy must never be despised or even belittled. However, the over-emphasis has contributed to a situation where many charismatic churches have lost the art of winning people to Christ. With so much attention on spiritual warfare, anointing, power and prophetic revelation, people – especially ordinary unsaved people – seem too uninteresting. In fact, "coming against the devil" within the four walls of the church is one thing, but somehow, talking to your unimpressed neighbour seems so much harder. So we choose the easy option and stay where we feel strong.

So much of the prophetic dimension I have encountered looks forward to a coming revival, days of amazing blessing somewhere out there in the future. "Tomorrow is the day of revival" I hear, but I read from Paul, *"now is the day of salvation"* (2 Corinthians 6:2 NKJV). Try telling a dying man that tomorrow is the day of revival! It would be like Jesus answering the thief on the cross who asked to be remembered when Jesus entered into

His kingdom, "Let's talk about it again tomorrow." This man had no tomorrow. Jesus' reply to him was "today". For a dying world there is also no tomorrow. Today is the only day it has to be rescued.

It is surprising to me to find that Jesus' hero in the parable of the Good Samaritan won Jesus' commendation even though he didn't have the revelation brought by the prophets. I guess he just read in his Bible that God loves people.

## God knows His own

Anyone who watches Christian television has his favourite preacher. You can choose between the high-energy ones, the soft-spoken grandfather types, the sitting-in-the-kitchen-with-a-cup-of-coffee teachers, or the if-I-weren't-a-preacher-I'd-be-on-Broadway performer. Back in the eighties my favourite was a world-renowned speaker who, in sixty minutes, made me feel indignant, made me laugh and cry and experience just about every emotion a man can experience. He made me hate evil, love what is good and look forward to Jesus' coming. Fearlessly, he took on single-handedly the wrongs in society, lambasting journalists, judges and anyone else he felt was promoting unrighteousness. It was hard to disagree with him. I didn't like it, though, when he began to use his programme to criticise other internationally-known ministries that he didn't agree with. Trouble looms when you get to the stage when you are right and everyone else is wrong. To say true things in the wrong way and with the wrong spirit is never godly. The day I stopped listening to this hot preacher from the deep South was the day I heard him say this: "If Mother Theresa doesn't repent of her sins she will go to hell."

Of course, the repentance of sins is the way into the Kingdom of God. There is no doubting that truth which was preached by Jesus and all the Apostles. The problem with this preacher was not so much the truth he was preaching but the spirit he was preaching it in. I guess he would have said the same thing about the Samaritan traveller who came to the rescue of a perishing man. It's scary how self-righteous one can become.

Sadly, but not surprisingly, sometime later our quick-to-condemn preacher was found in a motel room with a prostitute and his huge ministry machine collapsed. Ultimately, it's not the truths we have stored in our hard disk, but the love we have in our hearts for God and for our neighbour that matters. That's what Jesus said.

Don't get me wrong. Right doctrine is important and prophetic revelation necessary as we move on in God's purposes, but I love one man's answer to an unsaved mate he witnessed to just after having become a Christian. Billy is your typical Aussie who has a clear and simple understanding of things. When he told his mate that he had found Jesus his sceptical friend said, "Listen, Billy, years ago I had a problem and I tried prayin' but nothin' happened." Billy, with the unfailing confidence of a theological seminary professor fired back, "You don't understand much, do you? There are six billion people on the earth and do you know how many are prayin' at any one time? Give God a chance. He's sometimes just too busy tryin' to get to everyone." Well, Billy still had a bit of learning to do about what the Bible says and right doctrine but, hey, isn't it great that he was trying to win his mate to Jesus!

## All you need is love

There is one more unexpected thing about the choice of the Samaritan by Jesus as the hero of the parable. In the previous chapter, Jesus had had an upsetting experience with Samaritans. While travelling towards Jerusalem, Jesus had planned a short stopover in a Samaritan village, but the local folk rejected Him and refused to welcome Him and His disciples (Luke 9:51–56). This prompted a violent reaction from James and John. To defend their honour they wanted to emulate the prophet Elijah by calling down fire from heaven to destroy that village.

Can you believe that? Because their Christian pride was hurt they were prepared to kill all the men, women and children in the village! They were Christian terrorists if ever there were some! Little wonder Jesus called Zebedee's boys "Sons of thunder". What is even more shocking is that they had just experienced the transfiguration of Jesus. One thing I have learned from dealing with Christians over many years is that all of our powerful spiritual experiences don't necessarily make us loving people. How could the men who lived with Jesus every day, having witnessed His glory, be so full of hate, violence and hardheartedness?

But what happened to John then? Because he became, according to his own testimony, "the disciple whom Jesus loved" at the Last Supper. And in the early Church he was known as "the Apostle of love". Well, I have my idea of how he changed. In 1 John 4:20 he writes,

> "If someone says 'I love God,' and hates his brother, he is a liar; for he who does not love his brother whom he has seen, how can he love God whom he has not seen?"
>
> (NKJV)

John is writing to others but I believe these words were said to him by Jesus to seriously rebuke him and question his love for God. I believe the apostle is giving a personal testimony of deep repentance as he realised that he, himself, was a liar because he didn't love people.

In choosing a Samaritan as his hero, Jesus showed how He was without any bitterness in His heart towards anyone, even towards those who rejected Him. What a great way to live your life, loving and not hating others.

The parable of the Good Samaritan is all about God loving lost, dying people. Since Adam and Eve, this has always been the absolute top priority of the heart of God. Any Christian who keeps this focus will never be out of the will of God.

Now, let's see what other precious stones we can unearth from this parable in seeking to be effective in sharing the Gospel so that others will listen and respond.

# 7

## Feeling for People

It was election time in France and all the militants of the various political parties were out in force distributing their propaganda. That's what I enjoy about working on the streets – things change from day to day. I was presenting one of my sketchboard messages where I speak about "the real you", the hidden person of the heart. Nearby the militant Communists were handing out their election propaganda, but I had the crowd, between twenty and thirty young people who were listening attentively to me. It was then that I noticed a fifty-something Communist lady attach herself inconspicuously to the back of the gathered crowd of young people. Forgetting why she was in the town square, this disciple of Karl Marx was drinking in all I was saying. Then, the most amazing thing happened to me. I literally felt the love that

God had for this lady. Imagine that! This person was promoting an ideology that allowed no room for believing in God, yet God still loved her and He allowed me to feel His love for her. Feeling love for unsaved people is so very important for an evangelist, otherwise, he is just doing a job.

In the Good Samaritan story the difference between the two religious men and the Samaritan was that this stranger, on seeing the thieves' victim, felt something. Jesus describes that "something" felt by the Samaritan traveller as *compassion*. This is a very strong emotion that always pushes a person to get involved. Feeling compassion is so important to Jesus that, in the magnificent parable of the prodigal son, we find this deep-seated response in the father when he sees his son returning home after months of rebellion. Jesus included the importance of feeling compassion in His stories because it was a personal experience that He Himself had on a number of occasions. As He looked upon the crowds, Jesus saw them as being in distress and discouraged, *"like sheep without a shepherd"* (Matthew 9:36 NASB), even though they had Jewish rabbis as spiritual leaders. Jesus often experienced a great compassion for people. He felt it when the crowds that followed Him for three days had not eaten and again when He came across a widow who was burying her only son. Because He Himself felt compassion, the heroes of His parables dealing with the lost and the broken have this as their primary motivation.

## Touching God

This is where the New Testament is so different from the Old. Under the old covenant, established by God with Moses through the law, God was simply untouchable. In 2 Samuel 6:3–7 we find an unfortunate event which is hard to believe. The ark of the covenant, bearing the presence of God, is being transported. Uzza, who wasn't a priest, is walking alongside the ark being carried by oxen. When the cart is upset, the ark looks like falling. Uzza puts his hand out to steady the ark and, for his attempt to help, he incurs the wrath of a holy God who kills him for having unlawfully touched what was sacred. Put differently, in the Old Testament, God just didn't like to be touched!

How things change in the New Testament! Not only does Jesus allow Himself to be touched by people who need healing, but He begins reaching out His hand to touch the people Himself in order to heal them. This is only possible because Jesus feels compassion for people who are lost and hurting. Compassion makes you want to touch someone's life.

Compassion for people, rather than condemnation, is a reflection of the heart of God. How would you feel if you came across what is common practice in France? Psychics set up booths in shopping centres. Shoppers stop and for a not insignificant sum of money, sit down to have their fortune told. If you saw them, would your evangelical spirit be filled with righteous indignation, rejecting both fortune teller and customer out of hand while quoting Deuteronomy 18, or would there be compassion welling up inside of you for a person who is unhappy with his life and misguidedly seeking help? In such a case, it's good to ask yourself the popular slogan, WWJD, ("What would Jesus do?") or how would Jesus have reacted?

## At last, I'm a winner!

When France won the 1998 soccer World Cup the knee-jerk reaction of the French was simply amazing. The night of the 3–0 victory against Brazil in the final brought over 1.5 million people onto the avenue in Paris called the Champs-Elysees, perhaps the most beautiful avenue of any city in the world. That very week I was running a School for evangelists in the Paris area so, on the Monday evening, I took all the students out onto the Champs-Elysees to capture the atmosphere of what was happening. I had already heard the predicted denunciation of soccer and especially the World Cup, as idolatry – the worship of sports stars, glorifying men and the obsessive pursuit of vanity – expressed by certain narrow-minded believers. However, what I experienced was quite different.

Back on the Champs-Elysees I noticed one young man on his own, leaning on a crowd-control barrier. He was looking into the sky. I said to him, "Are you happy?" "Oh, yes," came the reply, "we won!" This eighteen-year-old from the housing commission areas just outside of Paris was, perhaps for the first time in his life, part of a winning team. So many like him come from broken homes where the father is unemployed, a drunkard and a wife-beater. The children fail badly at school and drop out, leaving any chance of a decent future in ruins. He is a loser from the day he is born in a world where everyone else seems to succeed. Then his football team wins the World Cup! Pride wells up in his heart. He now has heroes to emulate, the stuff that allows a young man to dream. He feels so good. This, more than anything else, will teach him values such as hard work and teamwork. Why can't some Christians see this? I was just so pleased for that young man!

When blind men and others cried out to Jesus for mercy, they were not asking for pity. Mercy is not pity. It's the ability to identify with people in need, understanding what they are experiencing and responding to them. Mercy and compassion give you a great sensitivity to people and what they are going through.

On one occasion Jesus needed two attempts before being able to heal a totally blind man. After laying His hands on him the first time, Jesus asked him, "What do you see?" The reply came back, *"I see men like trees"* (Mark 8:24 NKJV). There is a form of partial blindness where we no longer see men as they are. They become objects to us. This is particularly the case in big cities where so many people occupy so little space. We live and move squashed against others. We touch each other all the time but the distance between us is great. It's only when you stop awhile and look at a person and wonder what they are going through, what they are going home to, what is important to them at the moment, that a man stops being a tree and becomes a man to the one who sees.

## Compassion, not condemnation

Even unrepentant sinners are just people needing compassion and not condemnation. Jesus showed just how different His approach was to sinners compared to that of religious people. When the adulterous woman was brought to Jesus, everything demanded that she be stoned. She had violated God's law given to Moses, broken her marriage vows, wrecked the happiness of possibly two families and been caught in the act of adultery with no evidence of any remorse or repentance. Jesus should have felt revulsion, condemnation or at least indignation. But instead He felt love and let her go with a stern but simple order not to start again. Sin provokes the ire of judgmental people when sinners should provoke compassion in their hearts.

God feels for people and allows us the wonderful privilege of feeling for them as well. I do believe that each one of us will experience some incidents, whether major or relatively insignificant, which will make us more tender towards others. Growing up in a family of six kids meant doing your thing in the midst of all the others doing theirs. We grew up often living parallel lives, more concerned about our friends than our kin. Yet, I remember an incident that opened my heart to one of my sisters. We were all present at a pool party and enjoying the different games and activities. A popular competition around any pool is a spoon dive. The idea is simple. You throw in desert spoons and each competitor dives down to the bottom and picks up as many spoons as he can before his lungs collapse. There was much cheering and enthusiasm when it came to my young sister's turn. She would have been no more than eight or nine years old at the time. She dived in but, unbelievably, she could not sink to the bottom! Desperately trying to go down, she flapped away with arms and legs but remained on the surface. Everyone laughed uncontrollably. Finally, she swam to the side of the pool and got out. She did not have one spoon and I was broken-hearted for my kid sister. For the first time in my life I felt compassion for her. I went to her and put my arms around her and said, "Don't worry, sis, it's a dumb game anyway." It was so good to feel compassion and do something for her and this has remained very vividly in my memory all these years.

## Driven by love

Hudson Taylor, the renowned English missionary to China in the nineteenth century and founder of a major missionary movement, put the same question to a group of candidates, all of whom wished to serve as missionaries: "What motivates you to leave your country and go to a foreign land as a missionary?" One of the would-be missionaries replied, "I want to go because Jesus told us to go into all the world to preach the Gospel." Another replied, "I want to go because there are countless millions out there going to hell, never having heard about Jesus." And a third said, "Because I want to serve the Lord." Others gave similarly predictable answers. When they had finished Hudson Taylor concluded, "All these reasons are good and noble but they will never see you through the times of great trial and personal suffering. There is but one motivation that will allow you to persevere when others go home. It is the apostle Paul's underlying motivation: '... for the love of Christ constrains us.'" Driven by love, constrained by God-birthed compassion, concerned for the spiritual welfare of an individual, looking beyond the physical into the soul – all these are the mark of a man or woman who truly loves God. The apostle John puts it so well in his epistles: the proof that we have received the love of God is not that we love God, but that we love people.

Have you ever noticed that the great verses on God's love in the Bible are not so concerned about simply expressing truth as conveying feeling?

> *"For God so loved the world . . ."*
>
> (John 3:16 NKJV)

The "so" conveys feeling.

> *". . . having loved His own who were in the world, He [Jesus] loved them to the end."*
>
> (John 13:1 NKJV)

Jesus didn't just love His disciples, He loved them "to the end".

> *"But God, being rich in mercy, because of His great love with which He loved us."*
>
> (Ephesians 2:4 NASB)

God doesn't just have mercy and love, He has *rich* mercy and *great* love. In Romans 5:8, God "proves" His love to us and, in 1 John 4:9, He "manifests" it. John is overwhelmed by the intensity of God's love as he sees *"how great a love the Father has bestowed upon us"* (1 John 3:1 NASB).

There is much feeling in these verses and it is this feeling dimension that I want to experience in my love for lost people:

> "Lord, help me also to *so* love the world and to love people **to the end**, being like You, **rich in mercy** and having a **great**

**love**. Lord I want to **prove** my love to them and **manifest** it daily, that they may marvel at how **great** a love I have bestowed on them. Amen."

Perhaps you are thinking, "How is this possible?" How can you realistically love everyone around you and feel compassion for everyone, in every situation? We would be just one walking ball of emotion! Getting on with our lives and getting the job done also means living in the midst of people without getting involved every time there is a problem. Yet, if we err, we err on the side of indifference rather than over-sensitivity. Our hearts naturally – carnally – grow harder rather than softer. Tenderness is a work of the Holy Spirit and while as an evangelist one does have to have a thick skin at times, one must never lose tenderness of heart.

Jesus felt compassion, whether confronted with the crowds or a particularly heart-touching situation. Evangelists need to feel for crowds and be able to feel for an individual. What stirs my soul more than raw human need is when I sense God doing something in a person's life. Perhaps they will express surprise and interest when they discover that I am a pastor or when someone makes a statement that is out of the ordinary, like one woman I met briefly who simply said in passing, "We could all do with a bit more spirituality." My compassion juices really get going when I see a person genuinely wanting to understand about God and life, when they reveal their soul to me. This is spiritual compassion rather than sentimentality. Isn't it moving to see someone begin to open up to the grace of God?

## Where's Freddy?

Such love and compassion really do affect people. When we first came to France, my wife and I were based in a church in the south, in the city of Nimes. When I wasn't travelling, I would preach in the church and on one occasion, a young man came forward to give his life to Christ at the end of the meeting. His name was Jean-Marc. After praying with him, I called over one of the leaders of the church to counsel him. Now, Freddy, the leader I called over, is a wonderful man. There's something about a person who is so full of love for people. Fifteen minutes after the end of the meeting, I turned and noticed Freddy still talking with Jean-Marc. He wasn't just talking to him, he was loving him, sharing his heart while holding the back of the young man's head with his hand. The following Sunday I was in the foyer of the church, greeting folk as they arrived for the service. What joy I had to see Jean-Marc arriving with a Bible in his hand. "Hi, Jean-Marc, how are you?" I said, as I shook his hand. Looking over my shoulder, he replied, "Hi, where's Freddy?" "Now just a minute!" I thought, "I'm the pastor! You were saved under my preaching. I led you in a commitment to Christ and prayed for you and all you can say to me is 'Hi, where's Freddy?'" It was just another indication that good preaching is one thing, but even more powerful is good loving!

And good loving was what the Good Samaritan did to the man lying half dead on the side of the road.

# 8

# Oil, Wine and Donkeys

Evangelism Western-style is bringing lost souls in one at the time. This requires a lot more personal involvement from the evangelist than if he just turns up at a meeting where thousands are present, preaches the Gospel, makes an appeal, prays, and goes back to his hotel room.

People just don't get saved very easily in the West. It's going to cost you your wine, your oil, your bandages and your donkey if you want to see a dead man come back to life. Nurses have the most incredible "people job" that exists. The surgeon has a person while he's under anaesthetic. He doesn't have to deal with a person but with a body. The nurse, however, deals also with the person. She has to not only ensure that the right treatment is given, but she must find the right words when that same patient loses patience or, worse still, hope. The evangelist is more of a nurse than a surgeon.

Hands-on evangelism is the only way we will have transformed people to show for our efforts in the West. Pouring in one's oil and wine on very real wounds, cleansing them and dressing them caringly is a messy business, but do we really want to bring dying people back to life?

Perhaps in another era things were different and you could raise them up by sending a servant with a stick. But when that doesn't work, either you get personally involved or you bury the poor fellow! I'm referring to Elisha, of course. The dead man was a youth, the son of a Shunammite woman. When in 2 Kings 4 Elisha hears the terrible news of his death, he immediately dispatches his servant Gehazi with his prophet's stick and clear instructions as to how to operate. Elisha, with great concern for the Shunammite, sets off towards her house. He's a prophet of God and he's sure that his stick ministry will be effective. But, it is a failure. The dead boy remains very dead, stretched out on his bed.

In this situation Elisha cannot use servants and sticks. He must get personally involved. Like a matador facing the bull in the ring alone, he enters into the dead man's room, closes the door and prays until God tells him what to do. He climbs up on the dead body (they would put you in jail if you did that sort of thing today!) A breathing mouth meets a dead one, seeing eyes meet eyes that have no light in them, warm hands are laid upon cold ones and something happens! The lifeless corpse begins to warm up. But we do not have a resurrection yet. The matador leaves the ring for a few minutes of reflection and Elisha paces all around the house, preparing himself to face death a second time.

He goes back into the ring and the bull is still there, snorting but wounded. The man of God stretches out on the youth's body again. This is literally hands-on ministry, hand-to-hand combat. Then it happens – the most incredible series of sneezes anybody has ever heard! After seven sneezes (things often happen in sevens when God is at work) the lad opens his eyes. There we have it. The life that was in Elisha has overcome the death that was in the young man.

The point is that spiritually dead Westerners don't wake up when you send a servant with a stick. Few of the evangelistic activities of churches produce genuinely transformed new converts to Christ. Bible expositions, concerts, evangelistic services, tract distribution and every other way of reaching out with the Gospel are all worthwhile events, but none can ever replace mouth-to-mouth, eye to eye, hand-to-hand contact. This was the problem for a well-known evangelical church in Paris celebrating 100 years of existence. The leaders wanted this to be an occasion to impact the local community. The magnificent Bible exposition was set up, full-colour brochures were printed and placed in thousands of letterboxes. But there was genuine disappointment and bewilderment in the pastor's voice when he told me that very few people came throughout the week. It's tough work competing with DVDs, videos, satellite and cable TV, computer games and the Internet!

## Give them what you've got

When the Good Samaritan found the dead (or half dead) man, he didn't give him an address to go to. He poured something into his failing life. This was no doctor on a house-call with medical supplies for his patient. The wine used for the wounds would have otherwise been enjoyed during the traveller's evening meal and the oil, such a precious and useful commodity, would have been used on this occasion as medicine. Let's not get too allegorical, trying to find symbolic spiritual meaning for the oil and the wine. If we went down that road, we would say that the oil is a symbol of the Holy Spirit and the wine signifies joy. Human contact is what is important here and the impartation of what we have and who we are. The Holy Spirit and our joy are obviously involved. One who has oil and wine pours what is his into the wounds of another. This is the way back to health and life for a dying man.

Giving first aid at the scene of an accident saves lives. Surf lifesavers are always offering courses to instruct the general public on basic techniques of first aid, especially for drowning victims. The number one priority is mouth-to-mouth resuscitation. Having been pulled out of the water, the accident victim isn't breathing. If he doesn't restart in the following seconds he will surely die. There is no breath in him but someone else's breath can give him life. The dying man is laid on the beach, his head is tilted back, his nose is pinched and the rescuer begins to exhale, sending air deeply into the empty lungs. Very quickly the breathing process is kick-started and another life is saved. Perhaps the idea of putting your mouth on another person's, especially if you're not in love, doesn't appeal to you, but human contact – even in communicating spiritual life – is vital. This is why Jesus healed through the laying on of hands and not simply through a word or a prayer. Jairus' daughter came to life when

Jesus took her by the hand. Peter was saved from drowning by grabbing a hand. Blind men were healed with a touching hand and Jesus' holy hands even touched leaking, leprous skin. An evangelist, if he is going to win anyone to Jesus, has to get up close to people.

Several years ago British Telecom ran a remarkable series of advertisements on television. Of course, as any telephone supplier will try to do, the point is to get people talking as long as possible on the phone. In each scene, there were precious moments shared between the two people: comfort, friendship, joy, concern and each time the punch-line was, "It's good to talk." Two people sharing life does them both a lot of good. This is the kind of evangelism we want. Not the one where I'm doing the talking and the other person just listens. Successful evangelism is based not on "it's good to e-mail", but on "it's good to talk"!

## Winning people who aren't hurting

Evangelical Christians tend to feel more comfortable trying to reach down-and-outers rather than up-and-outers. When someone has made a mess of his life or has endured hardship and suffering, we feel we have the answer to his or her unhappiness. "Come to Jesus," we say, "and you will experience love, peace and joy." This, of course, is absolutely true. However, when the would-be evangelist is confronted with someone who is happy without Jesus, he is often disorientated because his worldview says you can't possibly be happy without Jesus.

It's quite amazing to see Christians responding to unsaved people who don't have specific problems. They are happily married, have a good job, the kids aren't on drugs and their health is fine. How often, when faced with a "happy-without-Jesus" person, the Christian feels that it is his responsibility to try to convince him that he couldn't possibly be happy without Jesus. After haranguing him about how he is full of pride and selfishness and convincing him that deep down he isn't happy after all, then he says, "But I have good news for you! Now that you are unhappy, come to Jesus and you will be happy!" It's quite a mindless practice.

People are not spiritually dead because they have a lot of problems – it's because they are estranged from God. Human beings are made with certain capacities in some areas, but in other areas, they have no capacities. We were not made to fly. We can flap our arms all we like – we won't take off! Man was not meant to live underwater. More than a minute or so underwater and you'll be a candidate for mouth-to-mouth resuscitation. Yet man does have a capacity to believe in God. If someone doesn't believe in God, it's not because man can't have faith – it's because that particular man doesn't have faith. It's got nothing to do with having problems. If you bring a faithless person your oil and wine, he'll wear your oil and drink your wine!

He needs something else poured into his life that is not related to problems, but has everything to do with spiritual need. Philip, our only named evangelist in the New Testament, poured understanding into an Ethiopian eunuch's mind. Jesus did the same with Nicodemus. Helping people awaken to spiritual life and truth, especially when they come from a scientifically-based education system like we have in Western society, cannot be problem-orientated but rather understanding-orientated. Pouring understanding into clouded thinking is a great challenge, but it's fascinating to see when the light begins to reach them.

## A scientist finds God

Stephane was about as hard a case as you can expect to find. A confirmed atheist, son of atheists, surrounded by atheists and successfully studying mathematics at its highest level, this young man seemed impenetrable. He was no "victim beside the road", needing to be picked up by a Good Samaritan. However, these days, on Sunday mornings, you'll find him loving Jesus, worshipping with outstretched arms in our church service. What happened? When he publicly gave his testimony he was able to identify four things that caused faith to begin to shine into his heart.

Firstly, there was his own questioning of scientific discovery. He had been convinced that science had all the answers. When he began to systematically investigate, he changed his mind. He came to the conclusion that science had all the questions. In fact, he realised that science was asking him to believe in the god called "chance". By chance, the world came into being through a "Big Bang". Yet, everything pointed to an incredible order in nature. Even the most basic cell structure was so complex. What could be behind it?

Then there was a friend of his, also a scientific-type, who one day turned up talking about the spiritual experience he had had. Faith was now part of his life. Stephane listened intrigued, trying to understand. An old, very old, street preacher also had his part to play. As a university student, Stephane had often seen this evangelist in front of the University of Bordeaux engaging amused undergraduates. The over-eighty, never-to-retire preacher, was a well-known figure in the area and could, at any time, appear on trams, trains or in marketplaces, calling godless people, especially students, to "Repent, for the Kingdom of God is at hand." In a satirical article in a university newspaper, Stephane wrote about this Old Testament-like figure. Despite the obvious irony in the article, you can read genuine respect for the man's courage in Stephane's words. Finally, what was to clinch the deal, was the fact that he fell in love. Yes, Liliana, a vivacious, young Colombian woman who had recently come to Christ herself, swept him off his feet. There is no doubt that when God is after someone, He always gets his man!

Throughout all four phases, what was being poured into this atheist was understanding and for the unbeliever who isn't hurting, testimony and personal sharing, reaching into his darkened mind is the way to go for the evangelist.

I enjoy it when I engage atheists who tell me that God couldn't possibly exist. "Do you know Denise Kelly?" I say to them. "No," they reply. "Well, it's not because you don't know her that she doesn't exist! I married her over twenty-five years ago. I love her and she loves me, so don't try to tell me she doesn't exist!" Any honest university student acknowledges that I have a point.

## An evangelist's donkey

How donkeys are important in the Bible! God spoke to Baalam through a donkey. He then looked more of a donkey than the donkey! Jesus rode triumphantly into Jerusalem on nothing more than a donkey and the beast on which the Good Samaritan placed the man was, no doubt, also a donkey. This is part of the evangelist's equipment which will be needed in bringing dead men back to life. The donkey was the link between the first aid given to the robbery victim on the side of the road and the nursing care he would receive in the inn.

Again, we have an evangelist's hands-on ministry. He is totally involved with this man's rescue and what he has arranged for his own journey must also serve those he picks up. The Good Samaritan accepts to be put out for the sake of another. He should be riding, but he accepts to walk. If he hadn't stopped, life would have been easier for him, but his conscience would not have allowed him to sleep peacefully at night. If the pleasure of sin is only for a season, then so is the cost of service. After that time is up, each one receives his eternal retribution or reward. It's a straight choice between seeking the comfort of this life in what one possesses or seeking the comfort that awaits anyone using his donkey to carry a dying man towards life. Wasn't it Jesus who said,

> "Truly I say to you, to the extent that you did it to one of these brothers of Mine, even the least of them, you did it to Me."
>
> (Matthew 25:40 NASB)

Donkeys don't mind who they carry, but God minds. Perhaps the evangelist's life would move at a faster pace if, after administering first aid, he went on, reassuring himself that he had done what he could. Yet, if we find someone who can't walk on his own, he must be carried to the next stop. We can't just leave people behind if they want to come with us.

During one period in our Paris church, a number of people were saved who were particularly demanding because of the needs they had: one needed constant time and attention, another much patience in understanding her suffering. Another little old lady who didn't know what a rhetorical question was would continually answer back in the middle of my preaching. God was putting us to the test. Could He entrust us with the poor and needy or did we only have time for the salvation of the rich and well? Caring for these wonderfully saved, but needy new converts released such blessing in the church as our love for one another proved to be genuine.

The Good Samaritan puts himself out so that a man can be brought in. A successful evangelist will do likewise.

# 9

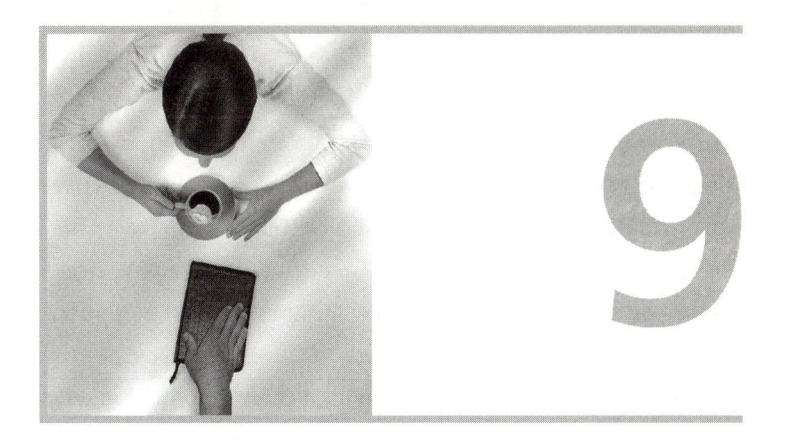

# The Inn for Injured Travellers

This most significant story of the Good Samaritan told by Jesus, raises some interesting questions regarding the relationship between the evangelist and the Church. If the Samaritan is the evangelist, then the inn is a local church. It is important to note that the ongoing healing and restoring of the robbers' victim would take place in the context of an inn. While there are several well-known and often-quoted Bible images for the Church – a temple, a body, a bride – the picture of an inn where an injured traveller can recover cannot be overlooked. Most evangelists will acknowledge that they need to work closely with local churches, but what kind of church does an evangelist need to bring people to?

In France, as in all countries, there is an amazing variety of hotels you can choose from, depending on what you want to pay. Bottom of the range is a chain called "Formule 1". You have a bed in a room, a TV and the wash basin and that's about it. No private shower or toilet, no tea or coffee facilities and no reception. Everything happens with credit cards. You get what you pay for and service is at a minimum. An injured traveller would quietly pass away here! At the other end of the scale, you have the hotel where they want to do everything for you: shine your shoes, press your shirts and in the bathroom, there are all kinds of exotic products to pamper yourself with. The staff is courteous and friendly, but once you've checked out, you're quickly forgotten.

Then there is the English Bed-and-Breakfast. They have a slogan: "You arrive as a guest and leave as a friend". The emphasis is on being terribly personal. Some really like this homely touch. I prefer the five-star treatment if ever I can get it! But all kinds of things can happen in English Bed-and-Breakfasts, like the time my wife and I went to England to speak at a conference in Exeter. We travelled a few days earlier to enjoy all-things-English and booked a room in a Bed-and-Breakfast through a travel agency. It was a lovely country cottage with farm animals and even a pond for carp fishing. When we arrived, we were warmly greeted by the lady of the house whose name was Jenny. That's how it happens in a B & B. "Hi Jenny, my name is Vince and this is Denise," we responded.

She was most interested when she found out that I was a pastor and very quickly the conversation moved onto spiritual things.

She was a faithful member of the local Anglican parish but, despite the many activities of the church, she felt empty. We began sharing with her about being born-again and knowing Jesus personally and immediately her face lit up. However, her cynical husband was roaming about. She had to rush off and we wanted to go visiting on this one day we had before moving on to the conference. "Listen Jenny," I said, "when will you get back tonight?" "Later in the evening," she replied. "Well, if you want to talk more and for us to pray with you, just knock on the door when you get in." The day quickly passed and it was now 11.00pm. Denise and I wanted to climb into the lavish bed. "That's it," we thought, "she won't come now." The light had just gone out when the knock came at the door. It was Jenny doing a very un-English thing – disturbing guests – but she was hungry.

After she had apologised ten times, we sat her down, pulled out the Bible and led her to Jesus in her own home. The next morning, her husband sensed that something had happened during the night but was too much of a gentleman to ask. This did not stop him taking our money, but what price do you put on a soul? Handing her a worship CD we had bought we said goodbye to Jenny, promising to pray for her. From that day on, we changed the B & B slogan to, "Arrive as a guest, leave as a soul-winner"!

We had found Jenny in her own home spiritually dying, but she would also need an inn which would minister to her.

## Understanding the church

Now, back to the inn for injured travellers. It's fascinating how Christians view the Church. Once you get beyond the previously mentioned Bible images, there are a number of other images which reveal how the Church can be perceived:

- ▶ *The cinema*: You pay to go in, look and listen. You either like it or you don't. If you don't like it, you walk out early. You have no commitment to return, but you may do if something interesting is showing.

- ▶ *The chess club*: You meet with people each week at a pre-arranged time to participate in activities that everyone enjoys. Once the game is over, you all go home and continue your separate lives.

- ▶ *The bus*: You want to go somewhere, so you catch the bus that will take you there. You are surrounded by people who want to go to the same place, but who don't want to know each other. There is nothing to do but sit. The driver (pastor) does all the work but the passengers do all the commentating and backseat driving.

- ▶ *The hospital*: You go there only when you're sick and you leave as soon as you are well enough to go home. Everything is catered to your need.

This fourth image is, surprisingly, the one many Christians have of the Church. It's a place for unwell people where doctors and nurses have one sole aim – to help you get better.

## Needs, needs, needs!

Yes, church is a place of healing and restoring, but it must never, never be a hospital! It is a fact that there are many fragile people in churches and yet they have everything, in theory, to become strong.

If Christian communities are seen as hospitals, it is because there is a need-orientated vision of the Church. God, Jesus, the Holy Spirit, the pastor, the elders, the deacons, the church secretary – they are all there to meet my need. One depressed Christian came to our church one Sunday morning, having spent years in what was basically a good church. When I asked him and his wife why they came to our church she replied, "Well, the other church didn't spend enough time with us." Isn't that a problem! How much time is "enough time"? One hour, five hours, ten hours, twenty appointments? With need-orientated people, enough is never enough. No, this man didn't need a hospital, he needed a vision-orientated church, one where he would lift up his eyes and no longer see himself and his past, but see Jesus.

Much ministry in churches is need-orientated: how to deal with our fears, our hurts, our bad self-image, our disappointments and regrets, our discouragement, our unanswered prayers, our problem relationships and our lack of confidence. Needs, past, present and future, will always make popular preaching subjects and lead to big altar call ministry, but what do they produce? When you add to that, need-oriented prophecy, singing, counselling, literature etc., etc., you do not end up with disciples but "me-ciples".

In fact, on one occasion, I challenged a preacher who was deliberately stirring up people's sensitive areas and presenting himself as God's answer. How manipulative can you get! Who does not have sensitive areas? We are not computers, we are not without feeling. If you touch me in one of my sensitive areas, of course I'll feel it, but that doesn't necessarily mean that something is desperately wrong with me and in need of "ministry". Perfectly-formed bodies at birth start accumulating all kinds of scars and marks from the various knocks received with the passing of the years. Jesus said that it was better for a man to get to heaven with one eye than to go to hell with two. Living with imperfection is part of maturity. When preachers present being perfectly healed and perfectly perfect in all areas of our lives, they are projecting something that they themselves are not and, somehow, people lose courage to face their lives as they are. We will never understand being perfect in Christ if we're told that the goal is to be perfect in ourselves. In fact, one of the great problems of hospitals today is that, while being nursed back to health, you can catch someone else's infection which can result in death!

## Changing in changing rooms

I don't think evangelists should be taking injured travellers to hospitals, but to inns. So, if the Church is not a cinema, a chess club, a bus or a hospital, what is the image that fits? An inn is a place of rest for people en route to a destination. It's a pause for a purposeful person, just like the changing rooms for a football team. The game isn't played in the changing rooms but on the field. However, the room where the team meets plays a vital role in any victory. It's where the coach explains strategy and motivates his players. The halftime break doesn't happen on the field but in the changing rooms and it is in that very place that the injured are taken to be looked after. The big difference between the changing rooms and the hospital is that care is given in the team room in order to get the player back on the field as quickly as possible. Health is not an end in itself, but an important requirement to playing the game well and helping the team to win. Christians, we often say, are not the spectators in the stands, but the players on the field, playing for a victory. Church, then, is a place where an injured player can be taken to, revived, patched up and put back out there for the sake of the team. It's amazing how quickly a football player can get over knocks when the rest of the team is still out there playing.

It really is a question of attitude. When my secretary found Christ in our church a number of years ago, she faced some major challenges. Her husband of thirty-five years walked out with another woman and years of serial adultery were exposed. Shortly after her conversion from a very worldly life where she lived only for her next exotic holiday, she began to have a serious sight disability which left her vision badly impaired. Her two daughters turned against her and she was struggling financially. This little lady was hurting. Yet, she loved Jesus and wanted to serve Him with all of her heart. She started helping out in the office, but she had to be handled with kid gloves. The slightest thing upset her and I felt insecure, always wondering when the next crisis would occur. We couldn't go on like this, so one day I called her in. "Chantal," I said, "I just can't work with super-sensitive people. In the Christian life there is a fundamental choice that has to be made. Do you want to spend your life carrying people or being carried? Every Christian will be one or the other." This had the effect of an electroshock for her.

That day, she decided to be a Christian who would carry others and not always look to be carried. Tears were replaced by laughter, the moaning by thanksgiving, and she has become one of the most delightful people I have ever had the pleasure of working with. In a society where everyone wants to see himself as someone else's victim, true freedom comes when you decide to put self-pity away and get back out onto the playing field. This, I believe, is what the Church is all about.

## What kind of church do you want?

The need-orientated church will be a hospital, while a vision-orientated church will be an inn. Choosing to be an inn may not initially be popular in this "me-centred" world we live in, but this hard choice pays rich dividends in the long-run, as people are helped to continue the journey towards their divinely-appointed destination.

What convinced me of this was my experience running a meeting for students in the late 1970s at the University of Queensland in Australia. On campus, there were Christian students from all of the different churches in the Brisbane area and I realised to what extent each church had a particular identity, depending on the emphasis of the ministry of the senior pastor. There was the worship church, the community church, the teaching church, the spiritual warfare church, the social action church. The very best students I had to work with did not come from any of these, but from the evangelism church. They were the ones who had some zeal about them. Prayer times were carried by them. They had faith for what God wanted to do and giving time and effort was not a problem. People mattered to these on-fire Christians and they loved their church and the mission to which they were called.

Of course, they loved the Word of God and worshipped with real intimacy, but their lives were simply not me-orientated. They were on the move. What I saw in those young people helped me fashion my understanding of church the way, I believe, God wants.

There is no doubt that a church where lost people are loved is a great environment to be in and it is into this environment that the Holy Spirit will lead people He is drawing to Jesus.

## Oh La, La!

What happens when the Holy Spirit begins to target a Frenchman? It will more than likely be a pot pourri of surprises, intrigue, romance, exotic locations and an unexpected twist in the tail. All this happened with a young man called Yannick. At just twenty-three years of age, this *enfant de sa generation* (child of his generation) had already tasted life's highs and lows. Professionally, he was well set, earning good money in computing. Yet, something was missing. Looking for meaning in life he turned to Buddhism, though not as some Westerners fleetingly do. No, Yannick plunged right into it seeking a higher plane where he hoped to find peace and inner happiness.

Partly to holiday with friends and partly for spiritual reasons he travelled to Thailand where he had an encounter of a different kind. She was an attractive Australian girl who happened to be "on-fire" for Jesus. They spoke for hours and

Yannick was finding answers to questions he had grappled with for a long time and, of course, there was something about this girl. Then it happened, he fell in love. Falling in love with a previously unknown holidaymaker in some distant tourist spot may, perhaps, seem to lack depth, but not for this young red-blooded Frenchman. When he returned to Paris he wanted to keep the relationship going. His plan was simple: go to Australia, find out more about her Jesus and marry the girl. For a computer man it was the obvious thing to do – go on the internet and check it out first. He did a search on "protestant church Paris" and the first to come up was pastored by an Australian (the author of this book). There was the magic word: "Australian"! So Yannick called and came to church that Sunday. He was ripe for the picking and when I made the altar call that day the handsome French web-surfer came straight out and gave his life to Christ.

In the very week that followed he came for an appointment to ask me a simple question, "What do I have to do to begin training to be a pastor?" I was stunned as this had been prophesied to me in America by the Rev. David Cartledge just three months previously. His words were, "God would send me a Timothy that I would raise up in the ministry." This is such a rare occurrence in France for culturally-related reasons. As I sat at my desk with this young man in my office, I flashed back nearly thirty years when as a twenty-one-year-old university student, I sat in a pastor's office in Brisbane, Australia, expressing my own deep desire to be trained for the ministry.

It never did quite work out with the Aussie girl, but God will use whatever it takes and now this young "Timothy" is learning to study the Word of God, pray with authority, share the Gospel with compassion for the lost and care for people. Such was his determination that he asked his boss if he could go part-time at work and applied to go to Bible School. His boss was perplexed, "OK, but what's a 'pastor'?"

Raising up young evangelists who will fearlessly and passionately take the Gospel to this generation must surely be one of the very great challenges facing the Church today. "Lord, send out the labourers!"

# 10

# Evangelists and Pastors Getting on

This most humanitarian of Jesus' parables throws together two very different men, a Samaritan traveller and a Jewish innkeeper making a living from the travel industry. It's a fascinating encounter between two men who would normally have no more than a purely business relationship. Yet things are different when we are concerned about finding and restoring half-dead people. Cooperation between ministries is very much a part of early Church history. Evangelists and pastors are placed together in that impressive list of ministries found in Ephesians 4:11–12. Together with apostles, prophets and teachers, they minister so that Christians can become what they should be in Christ. Yet the problem for the evangelist is that unlike the other ministries, his environment must be principally a non-Christian one. In fact, no one will ever become an evangelist if he does not choose to live and work in the midst of unsaved people.

The only specifically-stated evangelist we have in the New Testament is Philip. We discover him initially as a local church man through and through. He lived in Jerusalem and was a highly respected member of the church there. His wisdom and Holy Spirit-led life made him an obvious choice when the congregation needed to choose men who would assist the apostles. There are no more details of his ministry in the church other than he was involved in the practical side of organising meals. It's not the kind of training school I would have imagined for evangelists! Yet, he did learn the importance of local church, team ministry and working with apostles. This would be vital for the future of his ministry as an evangelist.

Pastors sometimes have trouble letting deacons become evangelists. The apostles in the Jerusalem church wanted to pray more and study the Word more. Philip, one of the key young men of the church, serving widows and solving practical problems, allowed them to devote their time to their own ministries. I can understand that they would not easily let him go. You don't replace a Philip easily. Yet, this young man would never have become an evangelist locked into the programme of the church.

The ministry of the evangelist is birthed in the midst of pagans, not Christians.

## Give me my Samaria

I was on staff as the youth pastor of a church in Brisbane, Australia, when I was asked to organise an itinerary for a visiting evangelist. He was a singer/musician and had asked for concerts to be arranged, not so much in churches, but in shopping malls, public squares and high schools. I observed a master at work, gathering and winning the approval of people who had not come to hear him perform. In one high school, a lunchtime concert in the school hall had been programmed and advertised. When the scheduled time came around there were no more than six young people present. I wondered if we should not cancel. "Cancel?" said the evangelist. "Watch this!" He turned the sound up very loud and started to jam on his guitar, playing heavy rock. Within ten minutes there were over one hundred kids in the hall and he had them in the palm of his hand. An evangelist just has to be out there!

What turns Philip into an evangelist is "Samaria". Persecution in Jerusalem pushes him out into a non-Christian environment and this is where he shines. He preaches the Gospel, since the early Church had no other purpose. God's power falls and the whole city is turned upside down. What a career change! Samaria made Philip and for someone to become an evangelist today, he will also have to find his Samaria, an unsaved air space.

The streets did this for me, not the church, but I learnt to cope with the peculiar calling of the evangelist as a youth pastor in a ministry team of a significant fellowship. Teaching was the main emphasis of the church and I had to blaze my own trail as a young man feeling the pull of the lost on my heart while, at the same time, learning to work with apostles, prophets, pastors and teachers. It was not the church that made me an evangelist – my school was the streets. They were my Samaria. It's such an exciting place to be and you never know what to expect next. My experiences as a street evangelist have been related in my second book, *Stories from the Street*,[1] and the stories continue to this day.

## No lone rangers

Yet like Philip, I understand and love local church and realise that evangelists must work with pastors and other ministries. We read in Acts 21:8–15 that Philip's seaside villa on the Mediterranean Sea in Caesarea became a meeting place for apostolic and prophetic ministry. It's a wonderful scene where different ministries interact. He was no "lone ranger" evangelist. In fact, we read how, in his first experiences as an evangelist in Samaria, Philip appreciated the involvement of other ministries such as Peter and John who helped him bring the new converts into the experience of the baptism with the Holy Spirit (Acts 8:14–17).

The caricatured picture of the evangelist who works alone, does his own thing and is accountable to no one has no place in the New Testament. So to whom can we compare him? Not to Zorro who fought for the poor against the rich, but who only had a faithful dumb servant and a stallion in his team. Not even to Batman, always accompanied by Robin in his fight for good against evil, but who otherwise worked alone with his real identity concealed. A more interesting parallel would be to James Bond. Despite his more than questionable morality, he has always been an agent of Her Majesty's government, answerable to a minister and a director and working with other agents on the ground to thwart the plans of the wicked, set hostages free and save the world. Well, perhaps, you don't like the comparison, but it's better than Superman, our caped-crusader who has come from another planet.

## Who is this innkeeper?

The Good Samaritan needed an innkeeper because his role was to carry in the injured, not to bring him back to health. This is the work of innkeepers without whom the victim will never recover. As an evangelist pastoring a church I have a number of different reactions from church members. Some are inspired by my example and get out on the streets with me. Others feel insecure because they don't feel comfortable with this upfront approach. One such couple struggled with this for several years. They were wonderful members of the church and had such a good spirit. They loved the church and greatly respected me as pastor. Yet somehow, they battled with the question of their place in the church. Their burden was home groups and sharing with new converts. Out of commitment, whenever we organised a major church outreach, they would be involved in street distribution, but didn't want to be thought of as one of my evangelists. The day I called them "innkeepers" a great weight lifted from them. That was it. I was a Good Samaritan and they would be the good innkeepers. As new Christians came into the church they would move in, appoint someone to follow them up, invite them to their home and to their home meeting. What a relief for this Good Samaritan! Everyone was happy and the work of God could continue to develop.

Innkeepers and Good Samaritans are different. An innkeeper is not a traveller. He is part of other peoples' journeys and must have certain qualities to be able to fulfil his role alongside an evangelist. He's a people lover and responds well to his different guests. This is a fast disappearing art as guests are becoming more difficult to handle. A pastor friend of mine used to say that sometimes he would just get "SOP" (Sick Of People!) I understand what he was saying but being SOP must be one of the leading reasons why many get out of Christian ministry. They love God, they believe in the Bible, but they have had enough of putting up with all the difficulties that people can cause us in the ministry. My innkeepers are the genuine article. What patience they showed in the face of heartbreak when one they had been following up jumped from an eleventh floor window and killed himself after a relationship with a girl went wrong; what pastoral care when a drug addict came off drugs and wanted to rebuild his life, or a troubled marriage needed to rediscover the joy of love. One young woman, a divorcee who gave her life to Christ, found it hard to be around others and felt she didn't fit in with the Christians. The innkeepers moved in and a woman found a family.

Innkeepers are never too busy for people, it's their life. They gear up their lives to look after them. Others have a house for themselves and their own loved ones, but inns have been built for a wider circle. Rooms and beds are made for resting and being refreshed but, when a badly injured wayfarer is brought to them, they can adapt and be a nursing home for the one who needs it. But the nursing home never becomes a retirement home. Sick travellers get better and continue their journey, making way for the next guests.

## Follow-up? I wish they were all like Louis

But after people get saved, what about follow-up programmes? Follow-up to evangelism can be a very frustrating and disappointing experience. Much time is spent trying to make contact with someone who once came. Perhaps the person came forward at an altar invitation, or had left his address, or expressed a desire to know more. Despite the promise to come or to come back, things seem to stagnate, so we send in the follow-up team hoping to see the person back in church. And then comes the frustration.

Innkeeper's can't nurse people who don't come. Follow-up is not about getting people to come back, but to care for those who do. There are simply so many negative influences on a person's life to discourage him or her from going on with Christ that, if they themselves are not very motivated to come to church, all the diligence of the follow-up worker is not likely to make a difference. If the victim on the side of the road refuses to be taken to the inn, there isn't much more either the Good Samaritan or the innkeeper can do about it. He will die in the very place he was left to die by the robbers. Nothing else can replace the willingness to come in the one who needs to come.

Let me tell you about Louis. At thirty-three years of age his life already seemed over. His drug-taking had started at age eleven and by seventeen he was a heroin and coke addict. Yet, he came from a good family, his father having his own printing business. What had they done wrong for the son to go so bad? With drugs came the usual bedfellows, crime and prison – just a few weeks the first time, then a few months and finally seven years for murdering a man in the Paris metro. By the time we met him he had already spent over ten years in jail. Doctors, psychiatrists and all kinds of professional help and support groups, despite their skills and good intentions, seemed powerless and when he left prison for the last time, his life was at a dead end. He slept rough having been expelled from his parents' home for threatening his own mother who had sought police protection against him. No job – who wants to employ a man who has sunk to those depths? – no money, no friends, no hope. One day Louis aimlessly wandered over to the local market near where he camped. Looking for something, anything, that might make a difference, there he met a man who had time to talk, who even wanted to talk with him. His name was Jean-Louis and he was one of my street evangelists. A real Good Samaritan in his own right, he had been saved in our church a few years beforehand and was now operating with a mobile Bible stand.

When I saw Jean-Louis he told me about the druggie he had met and hoped that he would be in church on Sunday. I must say I was surprised when, true to his word, Louis arrived, a little late and sat right at the back. That Sunday the altar call was unforgettable! Louis came running out and threw himself into my arms, sobbing uncontrollably. I felt that this was more than a drug addict regretting a wasted life. A miracle was happening in my very arms. Jesus was washing this man's soul, mind and body. Jean-Louis took Louis to the inn and now we introduced him to the "innkeepers". Everyone was overwhelmed. Louis was overwhelmed about us and we were overwhelmed about him and all of us were overwhelmed about Jesus and the depth of His love! Shortly after this initial experience, he completely came off drugs and began to attend every meeting possible, reading verses of Scripture in the Bible study and praying with all his might in the prayer meeting in the period leading up to his baptism. He only knew one thing: Jesus had saved him and he wanted to share it with others. One evening he took out a bundle of invitations to church and handed them out in front of a cinema. As a result of his own personal outreach that evening we have a beautiful young couple saved and in church. The irony here is that the young man he brought back is a highly qualified computer engineer and is deeply grateful to Louis for what he has done for him. The weak has become strong and the poor has become rich. And God, after 2,000 years, still uses the foolish things of this world to confound the wise.

Five months after Louis' conversion his father wanted to meet me. When he came to my office, he took me by the shoulders and embraced me. "What no doctor, no social worker, no professional help was able to do from my son, you people have done. You have brought an end to twenty-two years of hell." Shortly after, Louis gave his testimony at a visitor's morning where his parents were present. At that meeting, his mother, still under the shock of what was happening to her son, gave her life to Christ. It's a beautiful story that is ongoing. It's one which has made us all see that Good Samaritans need good innkeepers, and life's injured travellers need them both.

**Note**
1. Esterman, *Stories From the Street*, Authentic Lifestyle, 2004.

# Who Pays?

The fact that the parable of the Good Samaritan is not a true story gives particular significance to the details that Jesus chose to include in the story. As is so often the case in New Testament passages, the question of money comes up. As a conclusion to this heartwarming narrative we discover that restoring an injured traveller to health has a financial cost that has to be met. So who pays?

In the Paris Metro we are regularly asked by people in financial need to help them out with *une piece* (a coin). Most people don't give, but those who do are touched by the situation presented by the beggar and might give one, or at the very most, two Euros. The cost of caring for a soul that needs restoring is considerably more than one or two Euros.

How very remarkable this Good Samaritan is! Because of the compassion he feels for the robbers' victim, he not only generously devotes his time and effort, but also his money. He offers the innkeeper more than seventy-five times what a person may give to a penniless person in the Paris Metro. This is not a token gesture but a real investment in the life and restoration of the victim. The crude bottom line is that restoring broken people costs money and someone has to pay.

Forget this parable for one moment. If we were to use our simple logic, we would say that the evangelist has done well in bringing someone to church. It is now up to the church to provide for the spiritual wellbeing of the new convert.

Perhaps the church has a fund specially designed for such a work. I would certainly hope it does, proving – through budgetary decisions – that the church has the winning of souls to Christ as its number one priority. A treasurer might even argue that it is not only a responsibility, but also a good investment as, once the new convert learns the biblical principle of tithing, then the church will inevitably benefit financially.

Jesus, however, says that for establishing young converts, it's not the innkeeper but the Good Samaritan who carries the burden. This would rather encourage would-be Good Samaritans to take up innkeeping! How often have evangelists become pastors for financial reasons! So what is the spiritual principle behind this?

## Parents are parents

The apostle Paul sees soul-winning not so much as a referral agency, but as a maternity ward. To the Corinthians, Paul said that he had begotten them as a father begets children (1 Corinthians 4:15). As a father he feels financially responsible for them. It is up to the parents to pay for the children, says Paul (2 Corinthians 12:14–15). This is most significant in that the Good Samaritan does not relinquish responsibility to the innkeeper, he maintains it. Bringing victims to the inn and caring for them remains the responsibility of the Samaritan, not the innkeeper. It's enough to make you not want to get involved in the first place! However, when you are filled with compassion, you don't do cost estimates first.

Paul says that parents pay for the kids and not vice versa. Seems obvious. So, are new converts to Jesus customers or children for the evangelist? In a world where some evangelists are working out what their generous honorariums will be, the parable of the Good Samaritan asks the evangelist not to expect support from the inn. On the contrary, it is up to him to pay for the care of the young convert to Christ. How could you possibly afford to be an evangelist?!

This raises the whole issue of how much we are prepared to spend on winning people to Christ or, as Jesus Himself put it, *"you are of more value than many sparrows"* (Matthew 10:31 NKJV). Yes, but how many sparrows is the soul of a human being worth?

## What are the possible sources of revenue for evangelists?

An evangelist may have good revenue because of successful business investments. This is the best situation possible, as he is channelling funds from the world markets in order to pay for the extension of the Kingdom of God on earth. But how many evangelists can fund their ministry in this way?

He may also be able to finance his ministry by receiving support from the local church. If this were the case, the parable would be reversed. The innkeeper would be giving two denarii to the Samaritan. The evangelist, in order to finance his ministry, may do as I have done ever since my wife and I arrived in France: send his wife out to work! Most pioneer evangelists who last have a wife who is prepared to do this. Okay, I admit that with six kids this may be a little complicated, but in our situation, with no children to provide for, a working wife supplementing a pioneer pastor's salary is one possibility. In the sixteen years Denise has had to work to partly support our ministry in France, we have seen some amazing blessings in terms of her work. God was most certainly in it, but relief came when she was finally able to stop.

Perhaps the evangelist will say, "I live by faith and trust God each month for my needs to be met." That's commendable, but can he also trust the Lord for financing the spiritual needs of the injured traveller? What spiritual needs need funding? This would involve any support that a person would require to become established in his Christian life: Bible study materials, follow-up workers and administrative facilities. Few churches are structured to respond to the specific needs of new converts in a systematic way. They are often asked to simply get involved in the normal church programme.

The other possibility is partner support. For over forty years, Youth With A Mission has released literally thousands of missionaries by asking them to involve partners from among their families, friends and churches to sponsor their ministry. To be fair, it is not certain how effective in the long term some of these missionaries have been in filling the innkeepers beds with lost souls. However, when family and friends believe in their calling, full-time evangelists are released. What works so well for missionaries sent to an overseas field could also work for evangelists operating as a domestic missionary outreach, namely, broad-based partnership and sponsorship. Many who believe in and love the work of God want to have a part in emerging or established evangelistic ministries. This also draws prayer support. When you invest financially you always pray for success. No one wants to see his investments fail!

There remains the option that the apostle Paul chose to finance his own ministry at times: tent-making. This involves working in your trade for part of your time in order to support yourself in your evangelistic endeavours. While starting our pioneer work in Paris in 1988, I financed our work through giving English lessons to businessmen. I must admit that I enjoyed the contact with this level of the community and I found it particularly interesting to see these men and women, so used to knowing everything and controlling everyone, having to humble themselves in front of a teacher and accept making mistakes and learning from someone else. Some just couldn't cope with this aspect of learning to speak English.

## Spiritual people holding the cheque book

The fact of the matter is that evangelism costs money and you can't ask people getting saved to support you initially. If we want to learn from the parable of the Good Samaritan, then the evangelist remains financially responsible for the spiritual development of the people he finds and God will need to provide him with a good source of revenue to be able to do it.

This is not at all illogical. Business operates on a simple principle – he who pays, has the final say. By taking on the financial responsibility for his evangelistic work, the Good Samaritan ensures that there will be no loss of vision in the work that he does. How often un-spiritual administrators in churches have thwarted the on-going spiritual vision because they are more concerned about bank investment than people investment. Or perhaps some well-meaning pastor sees evangelism as something young people should do to let off a bit of steam. An evangelist who depends on such people for his support will feel like the beggar in the Paris Metro pleading for a coin. Who wants to live like that!

Money matters must stay in the hands of spiritual, visionary people. If your treasurer or elders don't want to invest financially in winning souls to Christ, change them! If your pastor doesn't believe that the spread of the Gospel is important . . . !

When my wife and I bought an old house in the Paris region which had received no care for twenty years, we bought a mountain of financial challenges. Now, I can paint a wall and replace a light bulb, but I also know my "Do It Yourself" limits. The work that needed to be done was far beyond just bogging up cracks in walls and painting over them. Some of the major repairs included replacing all the windows with double glazing, replacing all of the ceilings which had serious cracks, replacing the heating system and all exhaust outlets for gas vapours, installing a kitchen and bathroom, replacing the entire front fence and gate as well as replacing all the window shutters. We needed specialist tradesmen who knew what they were doing and they would need to be paid. Now, you can take the approach of some reckless believers and contract tradesmen, believing God that when you get the bill, the money will be supernaturally deposited in your account, or you can plan ahead to be able to finance the project. In Jesus' parable the innkeeper is no more than a sub-contractor. It's true that, more than once, God has unexpectedly and wonderfully provided at times when we were tight financially, but I've also learned to plan ahead. If we really believe that God has called us to preach the Gospel and win people to Christ, then the money question must be addressed.

## The bottom line

You can't initially count on it but, who knows, perhaps the unfortunate traveller will be grateful and will want to support the work of the Good Samaritan. It wouldn't take many grateful people, the fruit of your evangelistic work, to provide the support needed to develop the ministry. Success is vital for this to become a reality. In any case, several financial lessons can be learnt from this parable.

1. In soul-winning, money will go out so funds will need to come in.
2. Spiritual, visionary men need to keep the control of the finances.

3. Evangelists can't sell themselves. They offer their services free of charge. If churches or individuals want to support the ministry, they do so without the right to control or own it. They remain free to withdraw that support at any time if there is a loss of trust. Spiritual accountability to other established ministers does not imply financial dependency. The two don't necessarily go together.
4. An evangelist's budget must include the care of young converts. Literature, Bible study programmes and follow-up are part of the evangelistic process.
5. We need more money for evangelists!

So my advice to all the readers of this book is: generously support financially your favourite evangelist, today!

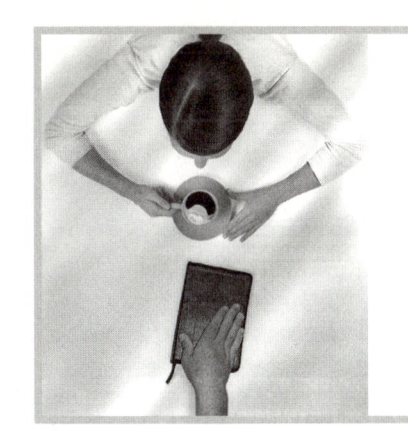

# PART THREE

## *Your Church Could Become a Soul-Winning Church*

# 12

# Your Church Could Become a Soul-Winning Church

It's an undeniable fact that very few churches in the Western world grow through people getting saved and added to the church. Baptism services cater, for the large part, to children of Christian parents and those coming from churches that practise infant baptism. Sometimes unsaved people drift in for a time and drift out again, never having experienced genuine conversion. Perhaps they were attracted by the bright music or the friendly faces. In countries where there is still a Protestant base, churches tend to develop through transfer growth with the flow being from the traditional to the contemporary style of church. Some churches get smaller while others get bigger, but an unsaved world is largely unaffected.

In Western Catholic-based countries like France we are blessed with not having the illusion of success that transfer growth brings. There are just not many churches or Christians to draw from. So we either win people to Christ or we die.

So much life comes into a local church when people come to Christ and become members. Everyone rejoices to see God moving in His Church. The pastor is encouraged about his ministry, the members are proud to be part of a successful church, the intercessors rejoice that God is answering prayer, so they pray more. There are more children in the Sunday School, more work for those doing follow-up, more money in the coffers, more musicians, more enthusiasm that only new converts can bring. When people come to Jesus in our churches we can all sing that old chorus, "I'm living in hallelujah land!" Amen!

It's a major problem then, when no one gets saved – or very few. So where does the problem really lie? Is it that our churches aren't good churches? Well obviously, there is always need for improvement, but if there is heartfelt worship, positive life-related Bible preaching, warm, open people and a reasonable programme, your church is a good church. People aren't getting saved in the church because the unsaved are just not present to be saved.

I do believe in the law of percentages when it comes to reaching people with the Gospel. When I door-knocked the area around our church in Ipswich, Australia, in order to win one family to the church, I had to knock on 100 doors. The law of threes is not based on any serious research, but I have found it helpful as a rule of thumb: to have one person responding to the altar call for salvation, there need to be three unsaved people in the service. To have one new convert added to your church, there will need to be three people responding to the altar call. Jesus Himself talked percentages when in the parable of the seed and the sower, only one quarter of the seeds fell on fertile soil, and of those some produced a 30% crop, some a 60% crop, and some 100% (Matthew 13:1–8).

So the key question we must ask ourselves is this: "How can we get a greater number of people who don't know Jesus into our services?" Of course, some would say that we should win people to Christ outside the services and bring them in having already found the Lord. If this really works, then that's fine, but experience has shown me that people who make a commitment outside the church context don't very often become committed members in a church. I am writing as an evangelising pastor who sees his church as his best tool for soul-winning. So, how can we get more people, who at this point are not "born-again believers" into our church?

The answer is not difficult. More often than not, people come to church when they are brought by a Christian. In fact, statistics show that over 80% of church members first came to church with someone they knew in the church.

So we have now reached a critical question on which successful evangelism in a church hinges: "How can we get the Christians bringing more unsaved people to our services?" The solution to the problem of few conversions lies here.

In a church where this is not happening and people have a culture of not bringing new people, it will be a major challenge to turn things around and will require more than one good sermon preached on the Great Commission. Two things will be necessary: *stimulating desire* and *effective mobilising*.

## Acquiring a taste for souls

Reunion Island, an overseas French territory near the tip of South Africa, makes the greatest hot chillies. In French, they are called "piment" and can be used to raise the dead, they are so hot! You can put them on just about anything and they will turn the most ordinary dish into an unforgettable physical and emotional experience. I love them! On my first trip to the island to help plant a church, I cautiously tried the "piment" and before long I was eating it like the locals. Of course my hosts were delighted to see this European enjoying their fine food so, at the end of each trip, my bags would carry several jars of homemade chillies back to Paris. From that time on my relationship with my fridge began to change. Whenever I was in the kitchen and near the fridge my taste buds would begin to water. This is the absolute truth!

Now that I had an acquired taste, the very thought of the hot chillies would stimulate my taste buds and produce a desire in me to eat some. I have discovered that everyone who genuinely loves Jesus has "spiritual taste buds" that need to be stimulated and it wouldn't take much to get them excited about someone getting saved in their midst.

When it comes to food, physical senses have to be provoked. The senses of sight and smell have to be activated. To get spiritual taste buds watering, the imagination has to be fired. This is where leadership must make some real choices. Churches so easily develop a teaching, worship or pastoral care culture. A soul-winning church has a soul-winning culture. It's the way meetings are run, the kind of testimonies shared, the subjects prayed for, the message in the songs sung, the kind of altar call ministry conducted, the spending priorities of the budget, the personal example of the pastor, even the question of the name of the church is important.

Lack of soul-winning culture was the reason for a totally failed evangelistic crusade I held several years ago in a church. There were simply no unsaved people in the meetings. The Sunday prior to the outreach, the pastor preached on women's ministry! Now please understand, I'm all for women's ministry, but not as a preaching subject the Sunday before a crusade.

Firing the imagination for saving the lost is a lifestyle and when ignited, there are some surprising reactions. I was preaching one Sunday morning in a church pastored by a man who was a well-known and successful evangelist. He was on the front row and I was preaching on his favourite subject, the impact of a personal testimony on an unsaved person. I was well into my sermon and the intensity was building. I stepped off the platform to deliver my poignant illustration: dominos. That's right! The Japanese had just established the world record for dominos falling in a chain reaction. I explained how they had taken many days to set all the dominos in place. The day came for the big event which would last only a few minutes and television cameras were there to capture it all live. A dignitary stepped forward and with his finger knocked over the first domino which fell on the second which then fell onto the third and so on, down the first row and back up the second. When the chain reaction hit a star design, many fell at one time.

Fast and furiously those dominos fell without ever missing one. By the end of my build-up I shouted, "And after a few minutes, because of an uninterrupted chain reaction, 250,000 dominos had fallen!" Then I shouted, "Hallelujah!" The pastor/evangelist on the front row, getting the point, suddenly leapt to his feet and shouted, "Hallelujah!" Then we realised that we were looking eyeball to eyeball at each other, rejoicing together over Japanese dominos while the whole congregation looked on, very amused.

Friends, imagination for winning souls to Christ can and must be fired.

## Stirring desire through preaching

How many pastors have made the mistake of trying to get their congregations motivated for evangelism by appealing to their sense of responsibility? "Jesus told us to go. They are all going to hell if we don't. If you don't want to evangelise, then you must change your heart." These and the endless stream of similar exhortations make the heart heavy and kill desire. I even heard one pastor say to his congregation, "Pastors don't produce lambs – sheep do – so go and produce them!"

Christians don't share their faith, not because they are indifferent, but especially because of timidity, fear or discouragement after disappointments and rejection. In our church meetings we don't try to make people feel guilty or impose something on them. Instead, inspiring preaching and leadership will bring healing to the hurting and faith to the down-trodden. The Word gives life which will seek to reproduce life.

This is how Jesus got Peter and his friends back out fishing after a night where they had worked hard for empty nets. Jesus gave them a word which re-ignited their expectation,

> *"Put out into the deep water and let down your nets for a catch."*
> (Luke 5:4 NASB)

The promise of fish from Jesus was enough to sweep away physical tiredness and despondency. Jesus ministered to them and gave them the desire to try again. This is where miracle catches are made.

Though motivation may have gone, the potential still remains intact. Preaching the promises of God puts back faith and zeal for God to move. Weary Christians spark up again when they are told,

> *"For I am not ashamed of the gospel, for it is the power of God for salvation to everyone who believes ..."*
> (Romans 1:16 NASB)

or

> *"Behold, I say to you, lift up your eyes and look on the fields, that they are white for harvest,"*
> (John 4:35 NASB)

or again,

> *"And I, if I am lifted up from the earth, will draw all men to Myself."*
> (John 12:32 NASB)

Hey, just quoting these passages makes me want to get up and go out again!

## Effective mobilising

Fired up Christians need to be managed well and zeal must be channelled into productive action. Paul, in 1 Corinthians 9:19–24 (the classic passage on effective evangelism), reveals his level of motivation as well as a very clear strategy to get results. With determination to win the more, he knows that he has to reach the many (percentages). To reach his objective, he does all things for the sake of the Gospel. He will run the way you have to run in order to win. This is one highly motivated evangelist!

Now for the strategy. He will not ask the unsaved to adjust to him, but will deliberately be very versatile so that he can relate to and communicate with all the different categories of people. Looking at the list of people groups he gives, the one that must have been the biggest challenge for him is the last one. Paul had to become weak to try to win the weak. If there was one thing that Paul was not, naturally-speaking, it would surely be weak. Yet, he accepted the need to become all things to all men for the sake of winning them to Christ.

Paul's strategy was to give himself every conceivable possibility of getting someone saved. Similarly, a soul-winning church's strategy must be based on diversity and the ability to adapt its programme and expression to those who must be reached. The programme will also need to release all the potential of the gifts and talents of the church members because, ultimately, we are all in this mission together.

Sydney, Australia, was built on one of the world's most spectacular natural harbours. You learn to love the sea when it is so much a part of your upbringing, as it was for me. I would often watch the weekend fishermen set out their store on one of the many pontoons which dot the shoreline. None of them ever fished with just one line in the water. Their purpose was not to just spend a relaxing time in the sun. No, they went to catch fish. To succeed they had to give themselves every chance. So fishing lines would be placed on the three sides of the jetty in the full knowledge that not every line would catch a fish each time. One line would be the right one, then later another would succeed. Sometimes one particular line would be quiet for hours before taking a bite.

As a fisher of men my church is my pontoon. I prepare my fishing lines and throw them out one after another. Regularly, I check each line to see if the bait is still on and the hook still sharp. I may not catch ten fish on any one line, but those ten fish will be in my bag because I've got ten lines out. The setting-out of my lines happens through the programme of the church and through committed church workers. We have caught fish through a monthly visitors service, tract distribution, youth meetings, Sunday School, concerts in piano bars, street meetings, advertisements in newspapers, home meetings, special events like New Year's Eve dinners, church picnics, healing meetings, Internet chat rooms, Bible stands in market places, mailing and quite a number of other activities. It's a big pontoon, so there's no limit to the number of fishing lines you can throw out.

Jesus makes a powerful statement to Peter, James and John – three fishermen whose fruitless night of fishing had been turned into a miracle catch. *"Do not fear. From now on you will be catching men"* (Luke 5:10 NASB). Catching men? Just like catching fish! Anyone can do it if he has the gear and learns how to use it. This is the role of the Church. It's Her calling and Her chance to be an exciting place to be in. Let's help Christians feel the same thrill as that of the five-year-old who catches his first fish.

## Producing evangelists in the Church

Forget designer-label suits, the five-hundred piece choir and the glossy flyer advertising the latest crusade! Church evangelists usually wear jeans, work alone or with a helper and make the most of limited resources. They aren't necessarily the ones who make the most noise. In fact, three of my church evangelists are the most softly spoken men you could ever meet, but they are out there each week talking to people, listening to them and loving them. In all three cases they have chosen the mobile Bible display stand as their evangelistic tool. It is non-aggressive and allows people to come to them. Another one of my core group of evangelists prefers the use of a survey to approach young people. He's a very pleasant man and wins over people's trust very quickly. Our lady evangelist prefers shop windows. She loves the contact with shopkeepers who hardly ever refuse to put up posters advertising our special meetings. Personally I like "in-your-face" street preaching with a sketchboard. My stories make people laugh and they often express curiosity and even admiration for the creative way I speak to them about life and faith.

Ultimately, if we are to produce evangelists in the Church, their way of evangelising has to be an enjoyable experience for them.

I've always been interested in the way Paul draws a link between the Gospel and the feet of the Christian. He initially got the idea from the prophet Isaiah,

> "How beautiful are the feet of those who preach the gospel of peace,
> Who bring glad tidings of good things!"
>
> (Romans 10:15 NKJV; see also Isaiah 52:7)

But it was especially Ephesians 6:15 which intrigued me:

> "... having shod your feet with the preparation of the gospel of peace."
>
> (NKJV)

What could this verse teach me about raising up evangelists? Shoes and feet, feet and shoes, hmmm? I looked at one of my shoes and suddenly I saw it! Why did I buy the shoe I had before me? The answer was simple – it was my size, it would fulfil the role I needed it to fulfil, it was within my price range and, of course, I thought it looked rather good on me. I chose the shoe for my foot because it fitted me.

Every evangelistic foot that will carry the Gospel to the lost will require a shoe that fits it. The foot needs to feel good and look good in the shoe it has on.

You've got my point. We're talking tools and means of expression. My wife Denise would never attempt preaching with a sketchboard on the streets. That shoe just doesn't fit her! However, leading a neighbourhood children's club she looks so comfortable and feels so good. Musicians love music, Internet enthusiasts love being online, young people just love young people. One young mother would go walking with her newborn baby in the pram. Cute babies are sensational tools for evangelism. All the ladies stop and want to talk. For another evangelist, it was walking the dog and for yet another, it was sitting in the same place on the same train going to work each day. Many people are creatures of habit and she was reaching those with that habit. Some like the in-depth conversation, while others prefer the short, sharp contact of a smile and a kind word as they hand out tracts.

Like going to the shoe store, producing an evangelist is showing all the shoes available in the store, asking him to try a few on and then deciding which pair he will buy. Afterwards, even if the new shoes require a little breaking in, he can do all the walking he wants.

Together with the example set by church leaders who reach out to the unsaved themselves and the promotion of a soul-winning culture in the Church, developing creative expressions of evangelism will do much to raise up and release labourers in the harvest.

# Honouring Evangelists

If you listen carefully to some Christians, you get the impression that "evangelist" is a dirty word. People who have tried to discredit me in the eyes of other Christians have at times said, "Oh Esterman, he's an evangelist!" or "He's a good evangelist" – the implication being that when you are a *good evangelist* you are a *bad pastor* or a *superficial teacher*. Being "an evangelist" can be seen to be about preaching and running meetings, but not about caring for people. This dishonours the ministry of the evangelist which suffers already a considerable disadvantage compared with the four other Ascension gift ministries of Ephesians 4:11. As he is called to devote much of his time to being amongst non-Christians, so financially the evangelist receives little support from churches and Christians who invest on the basis of "What's in it for me?"

Yet, without evangelists, we would not love Jesus as we do today and many churches would not exist.

Jesus made a very interesting statement about prophets:

> *"He who receives a prophet in the name of a prophet shall receive a prophet's reward."*
>
> (Matthew 10:41 NKJV)

He was, in fact, saying that if we want to have a prophetic voice calling us ever upwards into God's purposes, the Church must honour the man or woman sent by God to exercise such a ministry. Receiving a prophet is to honour him and the calling he embodies. The apostle John honours John the Baptist with the simple phrase, *"There was a man sent from God, whose name was John"* (John 1:6 NKJV). He is not just a godly man but one that God has *sent*. The promise that Jesus makes is to those who recognise this divinely-sent messenger for what he is and who honour him in his earthly commission. Those that do honour the man sent from God will receive a reward that is directly linked to the ministry gifting. So a prophet's reward is a prophetic promise that supernaturally comes to pass. There is no better example of this than in 2 Kings 4:8–17 with Elisha and the Shunammite woman. She understands who this traveller is and wants to minister to him with food and lodging because by doing this, she honours God. The prophet's reward, in this case, was a prophetic word about bearing a son, despite her old age and her barrenness. The following year she had her son.

The truth is that God stands behind the men and women He sends.

This principle obviously does not only apply to prophets, but to all the ministries that have been dispatched from heaven. I believe there is an apostle's reward for those who receive an apostle in the name of an apostle, a pastor's reward for those who receive a pastor in the name of a pastor, a teacher's reward for those who receive a teacher in the name of a teacher and, yes, I believe there exists an evangelist's reward from those who receive an evangelist in the name of an evangelist.

## The evangelist's reward

And what is the evangelist's reward you may ask? Souls saved and many of them! Videos of the massive evangelistic campaigns conducted by Reinhard Bonnke in Africa in his drive from Cape Town to Cairo bear testimony to a reward received from God because of the way our African brothers received the man sent from God. Charismatic Christians tend to honour prophets more than they do evangelists. In fact, oftentimes we have been poorly looked after while conducting a mission for a church. I'll never forget how on one occasion, rather than put us in a hotel room, a church asked a young couple in the fellowship to accommodate my wife and me. The young couple did what they could for us with the limited space they had in their small one-bedroom apartment. We slept in the lounge room on the convertible lounge suite which, when opened, occupied the whole room. In the middle of the night I felt the mattress move and I awoke startled. There was the young man climbing over us to get to the toilet situated next to the entrance! When he saw that I was awake he smiled kindly and said, "Sorry! Are you having a good night's sleep?" We had to wait a few minutes for him to do the return journey before trying to get back to sleep. The problem was not the young couple, but the leadership of the church who didn't honour evangelists.

What a contrast to the spirit of the people in a church in Nimes in the south of France that invited me to come as an evangelist and set up a base in their church to move out from there in itinerant ministry. When we decided to move to Paris to plant churches, the fellowship in Nimes put on a special farewell service for us. The pastor, with whom I had worked well, did the unthinkable at one moment in the programme. He asked for all those who had been saved under my ministry during those eighteen months to stand up. I didn't dare look around initially for fear that there may be no one standing and face the possibility that I had no fruit to show from my work. When I did finally turn around, I was staggered to see around forty people standing. I believe the church had received an evangelist's reward for the way they honoured Denise and me in our time there.

Men and women evangelists who win souls are gifts from God and when valued as such, will bring a reward to those who understand who they are.

## Some remarkable men

Church history has yielded some amazing evangelists whose ministries have left indelible marks on their generations. I have had the privilege of being exposed to some of the great contemporary evangelists, such as Billy Graham who has remained for all evangelists of every nation, the model of untainted integrity and faithfulness in ministry. It makes you feel good when your heroes don't disappoint you. I remember a workshop I attended with Grady Wilson on the occasion of "Amsterdam '86", the Congress for World Evangelists sponsored by the Billy Graham Association. Grady Wilson, who has since gone to his heavenly reward, was Billy Graham's associate evangelist who would step in if, for some reason, Billy couldn't preach. This old man sitting on a stool, having come to Amsterdam against his doctor's advice, had us enthralled as he talked about "Mr Graham", as he called him. The theme of the workshop was "The lessons we've learned in forty years". It was a holy moment and everyone present sensed it. So when this man of God would finish sharing his thoughts, someone would ask another question – any question – just to get him talking again. I'll never forget Grady Wilson saying, "Mr Graham is a wonderful man of God and I have had the great privilege of being alongside him all these years." But we all know that, don't we? Commentators all agree that one of the reasons for the incredible success of Billy Graham's ministry has been the six men who worked together with great respect, honour and friendship for over fifty years.

Another man of God, a mighty evangelist who greatly influenced my life and ministry, was Frank Houston from New Zealand. Houston? Doesn't that name ring a bell? In fact, Frank Houston is the real story behind the worldwide success of the Hillsong music and ministry out of Sydney, Australia. Frank, having been the general-superintendent of the Assemblies of

God in New Zealand, saw the city of Sydney one night in a vision. In the early 1970s Sydney was a spiritual wasteland with churches being small, lacking in life and momentum. Such was the spiritual poverty of the city that when I was baptised with the Holy Spirit in January 1974 in a charismatic conference in Canberra, I left my hometown of Sydney and moved to Brisbane where a real move of the Spirit was taking place.

Then along came God's man, the evangelist. Frank and Hazel Houston moved to Australia with their family in the mid-1970s in response to the heavenly vision. Their son Brian, who has become a Christian household name throughout the world, is pastor of Hillsong Church, Sydney. Successful evangelists should never forget the secret of their success – contact with unsaved people – so when the Houston family arrived in Sydney, back to the streets they went, to distribute invitations to attend the very first service. Nineteen people turned up, if I have my facts right, and what was to become "Hillsong Australia" was born. The name of the church originally was Christian Life Centre Sydney and from the very beginning, young people were saved – and not just one or two of them! Musicians from well-known rock bands came to church and were swept into the Kingdom of God. Right from the early days, music – great music – and contemporary worship would be the hallmark of the Hills phenomenon. Perhaps people are familiar with names such as Brian Houston and Darlene Zschech, but it all began when, at fifty-six years of age, a man of God from New Zealand came to Sydney and started again. As I write this I have learned of Frank Houston's passing into eternity. With sadness, yet with gratitude to God and to this wonderful man, I pay this tribute.

There is one more evangelist that I would like to mention by name – Carlos Annacondia, from Argentina. Having heard of the way God had mightily used him in the 1980s to spark the Argentinian revival following the Falklands War, I was very interested in trying to get him to come to Paris for a crusade. The first time I heard him preach was in September 1999 in Buenos Aires. On the platform, in full flight, he was a lion raging against "Satanas" and setting free all who were oppressed. Then he would move down among the people who had rushed forward to be prayed for. The lion would become a lamb and authority gave place to gentleness and compassion. This successful businessman, turned evangelist immediately after getting saved, brought hope to a nation humiliated by war and disillusioned with institutional religion. Our crusade with him in a huge tent erected in the heart of Paris, remains one of the highlights of my Christian experience. The first meeting was incredible. It had been raining all morning but at the very moment he got up to preach, the rain came down so heavily that it was difficult to hear him, even with the powerful sound system we had in place. This gave new meaning to the devil's name in the Bible, *"the prince of the power of the air"* (Ephesians 2:2 NASB). Carlos Annacondia later joked with us that bad weather follows him around. It is said of him that he travels with his Bible and gumboots. As the organiser of the crusade, I was involved in many practical details. However, on the Friday night, I decided to get another angle on what was happening in the meetings. Right at the back of the stand I found a great place to view the crowd. As this remarkable evangelist preached and took authority over evil spirits, I could see waves of the anointing of the Holy Spirit moving over the people, from the left side, down the centre and back up the right side. When the altar calls were made, hundreds would respond each meeting and on the final night of the nine-day crusade, there was standing room only as more than 6,000 people crammed into the tent. We had all received an evangelist's reward.

## Heroes of faith

Evangelists are heroes of faith and I want to honour them all. Not just the high-profile ones, but also the anonymous ones, working the streets of the cities of the world or going out into the more remote places. I applaud these men, women and young people of all nationalities who have responded to the same heavenly call that the apostle Paul heard, those awesome life-defining words of Jesus to him on the road to Damascus,

> *"Get up and stand on your feet; for this purpose I have appeared to you, to appoint you a minister and a witness ... to open their eyes so that they may turn from darkness to light and from the dominion of Satan to God, that they may receive forgiveness of sins and an inheritance among those who have been sanctified by faith in Me."*
>
> (Acts 26:16, 18 NASB)

The names of all such evangelists belong in God's Hall of Fame. For the sake of the Gospel they have accepted opposition, personal attacks on their integrity, being misunderstood, ridiculed, suffering tiredness, failure and sacrifice in order that, by every means possible, their generation might receive the ageless message of salvation in Jesus Christ. They are those of whom Hebrews says, *"men of whom the world was not worthy"* (Hebrews 11:38 NASB), but of whom it is written, *"God is not ashamed to be called their God"* (Hebrews 11:16).

I applaud these evangelists and I thank God for them all. Because they preached the Gospel and took it to the very ends of the earth, even to Australia, I was able to hear about Jesus' love for me and be saved forever.

## About the author

Born in 1954 in Sydney, Australia to French parents, Vince had a life-changing experience of Christ at the age of fifteen which imparted to him a deep sense of calling to the ministry. Four years later in January 1974 he was baptised with the Holy Spirit at a charismatic conference in Canberra.

After completing a Bachelor of Arts degree in Religious Studies at the University of Queensland, Vince went into full-time ministry joining a significant church in Brisbane. It was there that he met and married his wife of twenty-six years, Denise.

In 1979 Vince and Denise pioneered their first church in Ipswich, Queensland, before moving to France in 1986 to develop an evangelistic ministry. After conducting missions in various cities they settled in the Paris area and pioneered a church in the southern suburbs. The church grew quickly and saw the birth of a new movement of churches in France which has been involved in the planting of around thirty churches. Vince and Denise are now pastoring in the Sorbonne university area of Paris in a church they launched in 1996.

Vince is an evangelising pastor. His first love is the streets and he has preached with his sketchboard for many years in the streets of major cities in France and in particular, Paris, where it is estimated that over 50,000 people have heard him present the Gospel in his unique, creative style. Over the years Vince has led many people to Christ who are vitally involved in church life today.

Vince has produced a CD of his own humorous Gospel songs in French and has performed in several well-knowm piano bars and restaurants around Paris. Author of two previous books, *Miracle Conversions* (Sovereign World) and *Stories From The Street* (Authentic Lifestyle), Vince travels throughout Europe equipping pastors and churches to become effective in leading people to Christ in a post-modern culture.

We hope you enjoyed reading this New Wine book.
For details of other New Wine books
and a range of 2,000 titles from other
Word and Spirit publishers visit our website:
www.newwineministries.co.uk